MAKING STAINED GLASS MOSAICS

MAKING STAINED GLASS MOSAICS

ROBIN M. N. JONES

STACKPOLE BOOKS

Essex, Connecticut
Blue Ridge Summit, Pennsylvania

STACKPOLE BOOKS

An imprint of Globe Pequot, the trade division of The Rowman
& Littlefield Publishing Group, Inc.
4501 Forbes Blvd., Ste. 200
Lanham, MD 20706
www.rowman.com

Distributed by NATIONAL BOOK NETWORK
800-462-6420

British Library Cataloguing in Publication Information available

Library of Congress Cataloging-in-Publication Data available

ISBN 978-0-8117-7078-1 (paper : alk. paper)
ISBN 978-0-8117-7079-8 (electronic)

♾™ The paper used in this publication meets the minimum
requirements of American National Standard for Information
Sciences—Permanence of Paper for Printed Library Materials,
ANSI/NISO Z39.48-1992.

First Edition

CONTENTS

◇◇◇◇◇◇◇◇◇◇◇◇◇◇◇◇

CHAPTER 1

INTRODUCTION

Artistic creativity can be much more than the act of making something beautiful. It can serve as a process of self-care, mindfulness, and fulfillment. Finding a medium you enjoy can result in anything from brief exploration to a lifelong journey of gratifying personal expression.

Stained glass is simply colored glass. With opaque glass the colors can appear bold and saturated. Transparent glass allows light to pass through, creating various effects such as subtle hues or electrifying rays of colored light. Shapes of colored glass can be pieced together using a variety of methods to form decorative works of art. Making traditional forms of stained glass may involve precision and special equipment, but mosaic stained glass can be a spontaneous and playful process achieved with a few simple tools. The lessons in this book are all based on variations of cutting, gluing, and grouting glass on different surfaces and forms.

This book is intended to teach and inspire crafters of all skill levels. Detailed information about techniques and materials is provided, along with step-by-step instructions. This allows the projects to be accessible to people with little or no craft experience or experienced crafters who are new to mosaic stained glass. More experienced artists and crafters will be able to advance to higher levels by exploring the Challenges and Variations section of each project. Choose one or more of the following categories to set your intentions for making stained glass mosaics.

THE NOVICE

You have an eye for aesthetics and like to work with your hands, but you don't consider yourself artistic. You may have described yourself with cliches such as, "I can't draw a straight line" or "I am all thumbs." You may enjoy jigsaw puzzles because you have good spatial ability or you like piecing things together. Perhaps you have tried craft kits because you enjoy following patterns, yet you feel something is missing. You would like to develop and convey your ideas and establish your creative style. Start with the easy projects. After you have a feel for the materials and techniques, follow the steps to incorporate your own designs and personal expressions.

THE ARTIST IN TRANSITION

This group includes those of you who have a foundation with drawing, painting, or crafts. If you have previous experience with stained glass or quilt making you may want to try something less structured and more spontaneous. With mosaic stained glass, your designs can be ever changing or set in stone (literally). Glass pieces can be moved and rearranged until you reach your "aha moment" when you are ready to glue. Once you have confidence with basic cutting and placement techniques, you can explore some of the more challenging design concepts offered throughout this book. If you already have some drawing and painting experience, you will be able to apply your skills to more complex forms of expression.

CREATIVE BLOCK

You may have a great deal of experience in arts and crafts, but you feel stuck or unmotivated. School, work, or family issues may have distracted you from creative endeavors for a period of time, maybe even years. It could be that you never stopped making art, but you feel you are in a rut and are running out of new ideas. The

best way to jump-start a creative block is to shift media and try something new. This will free you from previous expectations to give you a fresh start with a blank slate. If you already have experience with mosaics or stained glass, mix it up a bit by exploring new design concepts or trying various combinations of techniques and materials.

IN SEARCH OF ZEN

Often life gets in the way of taking care of ourselves. You may feel busy or stressed, with no time for yourself. Living through a pandemic may add feelings of loss and isolation. Everyone needs time for self-care and mindfulness. A craft can bring focus and calmness into your life. Mindfulness means to be present in the moment without judgment. For you, nipping and piecing glass might be a process that quiets your mind and body. Glass nipping offers a physical release of energy. Some find the act of snapping glass to be gratifying. Piecing glass provides you the

opportunity to explore without judgment but offers something more personal than a jigsaw puzzle or coloring page. Allow yourself to focus on the present moment as the process unfolds. There is no right or wrong way to piece together glass. Simply observe and rearrange to find pleasing combinations. Embrace accidents and see where they take you. Notice how exploring and creating affects all of your senses. Be careful, you may enter a zone where you lose all track of time!

How to Use This Book

The projects in this book progress from basic to more challenging. Each project is presented with straightforward instructions followed by a section of challenges and variations. This provides a format of fluidity. Set your intention and begin at your level of comfort and experience. Move in any direction through the book to inspire, simplify, or challenge your mosaic making process.

CHAPTER 2

MATERIALS AND TECHNIQUES

Creating an Organized and Safe Work Environment

The first step to working productively is to choose and organize your workspace. The most ideal place would be a room, a portion of a garage, or a space in your basement designated as a craft area. This would enable you to leave your work out while in progress and have your materials easily accessible. Whether you have this amount of space or not, it is important to consider aspects of safety and organization.

I have the luxury of having a separate art room in my basement. When I started working with glass, I used this room to run art classes and as a studio to work on projects for myself at the same time. I had to swap out my materials for class materials, often using various media. Eager to begin my new craft, I did not take the time to reorganize this space (Figures 2.1 and 2.2). I left sheets of glass wrapped in newspaper or stacked in boxes and had to unwrap everything to find the colors I was looking for. I would dump scraps of accumulated glass into buckets and boxes without sorting them by color or size. My tools were thrown in drawers mixed with other things. I didn't want to take away from my work time to get organized and often had to stash things away

Figure 2.1, Figure 2.2 Before: unorganized space

Figure 2.3, Figure 2.4 After: organized and easy to use

quickly to clean up the space for my students. This wasted time when I set out to work again and couldn't find anything. I became frustrated and sloppy. I had more than enough space for my glass work and other art materials, so I decided to start from scratch and reorganize the entire room. This process took me an entire day, but I am now a happy crafter (Figures 2.3 and 2.4).

Choose a space or room that has a hard floor rather than carpet. When nipping or cutting glass, small shards and bits may shoot into the room and frequently end up on the floor or other surfaces. You want to be able to thoroughly sweep or vacuum the room after use. A drop cloth might not help with tiny splinters. If you only have a small portion of a room, position yourself so you are nipping toward a corner or wall, limiting the distance where the glass will fall.

The room should be well ventilated, as adhesives can emit fumes.

It is ideal to have fixed cabinets or shelves to store your materials (Figure 2.5). If you have to store supplies in another place after working, organize them in plastic bins. Similar types of glass pieces can be put in smaller bins and trays. Ziplock bags work great for keeping colors separated (Figure 2.6). Smaller bins can be stored in one large plastic bin.

Figure 2.5 Shelves are best for storing large pieces of glass.

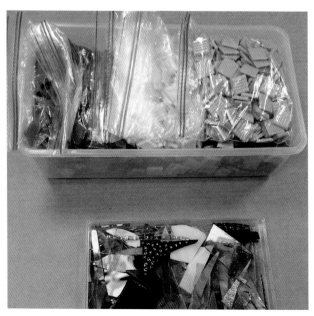

Figure 2.6 Plastic bags and bins work well for storing small pieces of glass.

To protect yourself while working with glass, wear shoes and safety glasses. If you already wear glasses, no additional eye protection is needed. You can wear easy-grip work gloves to avoid cuts. I like to work with my bare hands because I find gloves cumbersome, so I will endure the occasional small cuts. Keep bandages handy if you choose this option. You should wear disposable latex or vinyl gloves when grouting.

Materials

Working with colored glass to create mosaics can be a process attained through simple tools and techniques to create beautiful pieces of art. While almost any small found object or material can be glued to a surface to form a mosaic, the idea of focusing primarily on the use of glass will allow for an in-depth view of how to use a material that has limitless possibilities for exploring color, design, and light. Glass is glossy, non-porous, and will not fade. Your work with stained glass will retain its beauty and integrity in a brightly sunlit room or outdoors in the elements.

GLASS

Colored glass comes in opaque or transparent form. Use opaque glass for projects made on surfaces that do not allow light to pass through, such as tabletops, frames, trays, wall pieces, backsplashes, etc. (Figure 2.7). Small vitreous tiles designed for mosaics are a great option for opaque glass. They come in an abundance of colors, shapes, and sizes with different finishes, including solid, metallic, iridescent, and mirrored (Figure 2.8). Tile can be bought loose in bags or in sheets (Figure 2.9), adhered to removable paper or mesh backing.

Figure 2.7, Figure 2.8
Opaque colored tiles come in a variety of sizes and shapes, and with different finishes.

Figure 2.9
Glass comes in sheets and tiles.

Figure 2.10
Sheets may be nipped or cut to create custom shapes.

Stained glass sheets are available in both opaque and transparent colors and can be solid, variegated, or iridescent (Figure 2.9). Glass sheets offer the opportunity to create custom shapes and sizes by nipping or cutting the glass (Figure 2.10). You can use opaque glass interchangeably with glass tiles on nontransparent surfaces. For windows, candle votives, lamps, or any other pieces you want to let light pass through, use transparent glass to gain the full advantage that light has to offer. Sunlight can illuminate a room with color that extends well beyond the window you create. Notice in Figure 2.11 how the colors from the stained glass reflect onto the risers in the banister. Figure 2.12 shows the reflection of the entire window on a perpendicular wall in the stairwell. The reflections change throughout the day according to the position of the sun.

Accent mosaic pieces such glass, beads, pebbles, and repurposed broken objects can be used as a focal point or an embellishment to your art. I designed the window in Figure 2.14 around a broken red candle votive. The white rays are made of parts from a strand of icicle lights.

I chose them for their transparency, shape, and texture.

The two floral designs in Figures 2.15 and 2.16 are closeups from the same window. Glass pearls add texture and detail to this piece.

Glass tiles can be purchased in mosaic specialty supply stores. It is great to be able to browse and become inspired by visiting a supplier, but if you do not have one in your area you can order tiles online. Large chain craft stores may offer some in limited variety. Sheet glass can be purchased from a stained glass supplier. Again, it is best to shop in person, but you may not have a store nearby. If you order online, pay attention to the descriptions of the panes of glass. I have been sucked in by what appeared to be great deals only to discover that I ended up buying smaller panes of glass than I anticipated because I didn't check the size. There are good deals on eBay but these are often scraps or mixed bags where you don't know exactly what you are getting. I bought glass this way when I started because I wasn't sure what to select and did not want to spend a lot of money. I had fun improvising and creating

Figure 2.11 Stained glass window

Figure 2.12
The light shining through window brightens the space and creates an interesting pattern on the opposite wall.

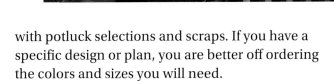

with potluck selections and scraps. If you have a specific design or plan, you are better off ordering the colors and sizes you will need.

SURFACES

The surface you choose to glue your glass on will be determined by what you are making and will be specified in the project directions. However, there are some general guidelines you may want to be aware of. For wall hangings, tabletops, and other rectangular, opaque glass projects, I recommend using cement board. This is a sturdy all-weather board that comes in quarter-inch thick, three- by five-foot sheets. It has score lines and can be easily cut to the size of your

Figure 2.13 Transparent glass takes full advantage of the light.

Figure 2.14
Glass beads, pebbles, and repurposed broken objects can be used as accent pieces in your mosaics.

Figure 2.15 Closeup of floral design

Figure 2.16
Closeup of floral design

project by using a simple hand tool. One board will be large enough for many projects and is by far the most inexpensive consumable material you will use. Cement board is available at any large hardware store or building supply chain. Avoid surfaces such as flexible plastics or metals that may cause glass to pop off. If your pieces will be exposed to water or extreme temperatures, do not choose wood, as it will warp or expand and contract. Use clear glass surfaces for transparent glass pieces. Keep your eyes open for old windows that can be repurposed and hung in front of structural windows, on a porch, or as a room divider. Old windows may be available from your neighbors who are replacing windows in their homes and can be found on Craigslist or neighborhood websites for free or a few dollars. Antiques stores sometimes sell old windows, but they can be pricier there. As you explore the projects in this book you will find suggestions for all sorts of ready-made objects that can be used as bases to make art. You may begin to see any object as an opportunity for artistic transformation by gluing glass to it.

ADHESIVES

Gluing glass to surfaces is all there is to assembling your projects. There are so many different adhesives from which to choose (Figure 2.17). The greatest selection and the best prices can be found in large hardware store chains. Mosaic suppliers tend to have less variety and higher prices. For transparent pieces you must use adhesive that dries clear and is nonyellowing. Some products are white when wet, but dry clear. I prefer to use adhesives that start out clear so I can see how the glass will look as I go. There is a white-to-clear adhesive called Weld Bond that is slow drying, non-toxic, sticks to anything, easy to use, and cleans up with water. However, I learned the hard way that it requires air to cure and turn clear. I used it to glue transparent glass to clear

Figure 2.17 Just a few of the many adhesive options available

glass. Both surfaces were nonporous so air could not get in. I learned from the Weld Bond website that heat and ultraviolet rays would cure it. I put the piece out in the sun for hours each day and after weeks the glue turned clear.

Clear adhesives may come in caulk tubes and can be found in the paint section of hardware stores with other types of construction adhesive. These adhesives are thick, flexible, and stick to mostly anything. There are some that start out clear, so what you see is what you get. If you don't want to bother with a caulk gun, there are plenty of adhesives that come in regular squeeze tubes and bottles that work just as well. Goop, Gorilla Glue, and E6000 are a few brands I would recommend. The quantities are usually smaller and more expensive than caulk tubes, but there is an ease to squeezing glue out of a tube that you may prefer. The consistency and drying times vary.

There are more options when working with opaque glass. You can use any of the clear adhesives, but the color of the glue doesn't matter. In addition to tube adhesives, there are tile adhesives sometimes called thinset that come in plastic tubs with snap-on lids. They may be found in the tile and grout section of the hardware store and can be spread on surfaces with a putty knife, or you can back each piece with a palette or butter knife. Plastic knives work fine for this.

The most important part of choosing an adhesive is to read the labels. Make sure the product you choose will bond to glass and your intended surface. There are different products for indoor and outdoor use. I may recommend something specific for a given project. Beyond that, you have to experiment to find your personal preferences. You may discover you need more or less drying time or prefer one consistency over another. Some of the useful adhesives emit toxic fumes, so be sure to use these in a well-ventilated area. I haven't found any noticeable differences in quality between brands but there is a lot of variation between types of adhesives.

GROUT

Grouting is usually the last step in your project and will seem to magically bring your art to life. Grout is a cement-based material that fills in the spaces between your glued pieces. It brings out the color of your work, smooths out ragged edges, and covers glue that has squished out from under your tiles. Grout comes dry or premixed and is sanded or unsanded. Sanded grout should be your primary choice for projects since sand particles have the ability to lock with each other to form a sturdy joint. Only consider using unsanded grout if the space between tiles is less than an eighth of an inch. It is a good idea to test or practice with a small amount of grout on a sample piece. I once ruined a window I spent weeks creating because the hardware store was

Figure 2.18 Grout seeping under glass.

Figure 2.19 Scoring utility knife to cut cement board

Figure 2.21 Glass cutter with oil

Figure 2.22 Grozing (top) and running (bottom) pliers

Figure 2.20 Wheeled glass nippers and tile nippers

out of my familiar grout. I bought something called "grout replacement" that the salesman assured me was interchangeable with regular grout. When I mixed the grout, I noticed it had a different texture and consistency than my usual products, but I moved forward with it anyway. The grout seeped under the glass pieces, ruining the entire window. It made sense in retrospect, since the product was intended to repair and replace grout. Naturally it was intended to seep. This was a lesson learned the hard way.

A spray grout sealant is recommended to protect your mosaics from water, mildew, and stains. Sealant is particularly helpful for outdoor mosaics or pieces that will come in contact with food or liquids.

TOOLS

There are only six simple hand tools required to complete every project in this book (Figures 2.19, 2.20, 2.21, 2.22). They can all be purchased inexpensively at a hardware store or online.

Other useful tools and materials to have available may include a T-square, sketching paper, acrylic craft paint, a black Sharpie permanent marker, colored pencils, sandpaper, caulking gun, sponges, rags and/or paper towels, table covering, tweezers, poking sticks, and repurposed plastic containers to mix grout. Additional suggestions for optional supplies will be given for particular projects.

Basic Techniques

Every project in this book involves cutting, gluing, and grouting glass on different forms and surfaces to make beautiful stained glass art. The following processes can be used throughout the book.

CUTTING CEMENT BOARD

Cement board comes in three- by five-foot sheets and can be easily cut into any size square or rectangle. You will need a scoring utility knife and a T-square, yard stick, or non-skid ruler. The board comes already scored in a one-inch grid pattern, which makes it easier to cut the board straight whether you are placing your scoring knife directly in the score line or parallel to it for cutting sizes in a fraction of an inch. Draw a straight pencil line if you are not using one of the scoring marks. Place the board on a table with one side hanging off a bit so your tool won't cut into the tabletop. Line your straight edge up with one of the scoring grooves or pencil line. Hold the straight edge firmly in place with one hand, press and pull the tool toward you with your other hand (Figure 2.23). Position yourself so you are not standing directly in front of the path of the blade in case the tool slips.

Repeat this scoring motion until you are approximately a quarter of the way through the thickness of the board. If you are cutting a large piece, you can pull the tool through half the length of the board and then rotate it to do the other half. It can be difficult to reach and pull through with one continuous swipe for a long score line. Next, flip the board over and draw a pencil line on the back of the board in the same place. You will be able to see your score lines on the edge of the board from the other side so it will be easy to accurately place your line on the other side. Score this side using the same technique. Then place your board at the edge of the table near the score line, apply a little pressure, and the board will snap easily along the scored line (Figure 2.24). If it doesn't break easily, score it a bit more and try again. The break should be clean and straight. Use a little sandpaper to smooth the edge as needed. Once you get the hang of this, cutting cement board should only take a few minutes.

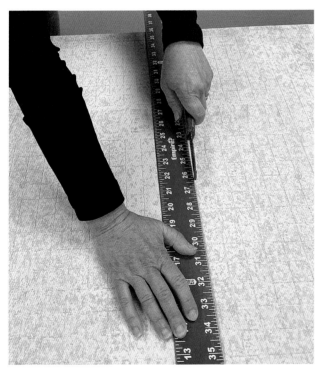

Figure 2.23 Line your straight edge up with your pencil line or scoring groove and pull the scoring knife toward you while standing to the side.

Figure 2.24 Place your board at the edge of a table near the score line to break.

CUTTING TILES

You can use wheeled glass nippers for all your glass tile cutting, but regular tile nippers are handy to have around for thick glass or mirrored tiles and are necessary if you decide to add ceramic pieces to your mosaics. Thick ceramic tiles or pottery shards can be shaped with tile nippers. For cutting small vitreous glass tiles you may prefer the wheel glass nippers, but you can experiment with both. Start by putting on your safety glasses. Select a tile and hold from both sides with one hand. For more control you can hold one edge of the tile with a firmer grip, but make sure you are aiming the tile down toward the table or near a wall because the shards will go flying. If using the wheeled nippers, position the wheel on the center of the tile and press the handles until the glass breaks. If you are using tile nippers, place the tile about halfway into the tool to press and snap (Figure 2.25). Most vitreous glass tiles are grooved on the back. When attempting a straight cut, I haven't noticed any difference in success whether I cut with or against the grooves. When cutting on a diagonal you will always be cutting across the grooves. The glass seems to have a mind of its own, so enjoy the irregular shapes and sizes of the cut tiles as they may not turn out as you intend them to. You will gain better control with practice (Figure 2.26).

CUTTING GLASS SHEETS

Being self-taught in working with glass, I began my experimentation with glass sheets by ordering scraps and small sheets of colored glass from eBay and bought my first wheeled tile nippers. My designs were inspired by the small irregular pieces. Before you nip, remember your safety glasses. Using the wheeled tool as described previously, nip away bit by bit at a piece of glass to get the shape you want (Figure 2.27). The smaller the nip, the better control you have. Keep trimming pieces to fit together like a puzzle. Save

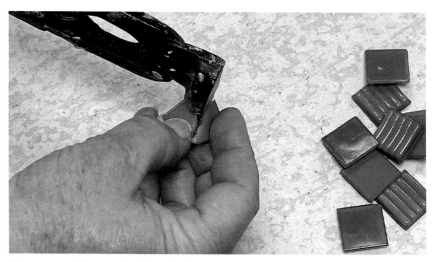

Figure 2.25 Place a tile about halfway into the tile nippers, press, and snap.

Figure 2.26 Play with the irregular pieces of glass until you find a design that works.

Figure 2.27 Wheeled nippers are best when working with glass sheets.

Figure 2.28, Figure 2.29, Figure 2.30 Faces made from scraps of sheet glass

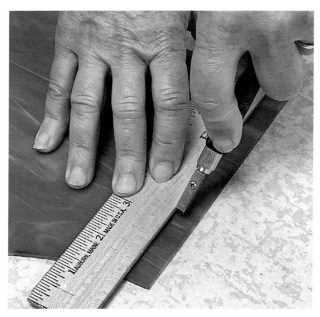

Figure 2.31 Use a ruler when scoring straight lines.

Figure 2.32 For pieces close to the edge, use running pliers to grasp and snap.

all your discarded pieces. They will fit someplace else. The faces in Figures 2.28, 2.29, and 2.30 were made from scraps of sheet glass that I modified with the wheel nippers.

Eventually you will want to design your own shapes from larger pieces of glass. For this you will need a glass cutter and oil. The oil provides lubrication so the wheel will glide easily over the glass in the direction you choose. Some glass cutters have a container that holds and releases the oil, but you can just dip the cutter wheel into oil before you score. A glass cutter doesn't actually break glass; rather, it scores the glass so it can be snapped apart. To ensure the glass breaks cleanly, only pass the tool over your line once. Hold the glass cutter in any position that is comfortable for you. Move the cutter toward or away from you depending on what gives you more control. Glide the wheel easily over the glass so the score line is barely visible. Then hold the glass in your fists on either side of the score line and gently snap the glass. It will snap easily over the etched line. Practice getting the feel of how much pressure to apply with the glass cutter. You will get acquainted with the sound and feel for the amount of pressure that will give you a clean break.

When cutting a straight line use a ruler or free hand to score the glass. If your score line is too close to the edge to grasp with your hand, grasp the piece with the running pliers and gently snap (Figures 2.31 and 2.32).

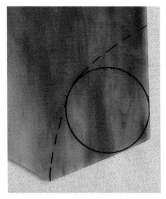

Figure 2.33 Draw your desired shape and cut the lines.

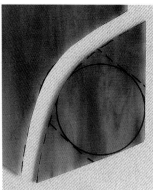

Figure 2.34 First cut

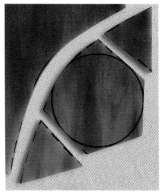

Figure 2.35 More cuts

Figure 2.36 Nip to finish your shape.

For any shape or line, you can trace a paper pattern or draw directly on the glass with a Sharpie marker. Black lines easily come off the glass with alcohol-based hand sanitizer. When cutting curves or shapes, it may be easier to push the cutter away from you to score. Glass cannot break along score lines that are at right angles or tight curves. You must gradually ease into the curve with a series of more subtle score lines (Figures 2.33, 2.34, 2.35, and 2.36). To break curved shapes or small strips, use grozing pliers. Use your wheel nippers to adjust shapes. There is no need to grind glass because the grouting will even out the edges.

GROUTING

After your glass is glued down and dry, it is time to grout your mosaic to give it a clean, finished look. Select a sanded grout unless the space between your pieces is less than an eighth of an inch. This will be the messiest part of your project whether you use premixed or dry grout, so wear disposable gloves. The advantage of using premixed grout is that it can be used straight out of the container. There's no need to worry about mixing in the right amount

of water or achieving the right consistency. Some premixed grouts contain latex or urethane, which improves adhesion and eliminates the need for sealing. Premixed grout may come in larger quantities than dry grout, so if you don't use the whole container it may dry out when stored and can be expensive. Dry grout comes in large amounts in paper bags or cardboard cartons, but you can mix any amount you like in a repurposed cottage cheese or large yogurt container and store the remaining dry grout for future projects over long periods of time.

Grout comes in many standard colors, but mixing your own grout allows you to add acrylic or latex paint to create custom colors. I prefer to use either black or off-white grout to keep things simple (Figure 2.37). Black grout is most effective for mimicking the look of traditional stained glass. It also brings out the colors of the glass

Figure 2.37 Black vs. white grout

beautifully. You might choose an off-white or other light color if your glass pieces are dark and you want them to visually pop. The rule of thumb is if you want your glass pieces to flow together and have a softer look, choose a grout color that is consistent in value and color with most of your glass. If you want the individual shapes and colors to stand out, then choose a grout that will contrast with your glass design. Also, consider how much you want the grout lines to contribute to your design.

Easy-to-follow mixing and application directions are found on packages of grout. The mixing directions are for large-scale projects, enough to cover a shower or floor. The most you will need for the largest projects in this book is a pint of mixed grout. Use a plastic food container that is larger than the amount of grout you want to mix. Fill approximately a third of the container with water and gradually add powdered grout until it peaks on the surface above the water. Adding enough grout will more than double the volume in the container. Mix the grout with a spoon or stirring stick. The grout should be the consistency of natural peanut butter (Figure 2.38).

Once the grout is ready to apply, you can spread it with your gloved hand or a spackling knife over your mosaic art. Squish it into all the nooks and crannies and wipe off any excess. Use the drying times indicated on the package as a guide. The time may vary according to humidity levels. If the grout is dry enough to wipe off, it

Figure 2.39 As you wipe off the extra grout, the beauty of your piece will emerge in full.

Figure 2.38 Grout should be the consistency of natural peanut butter.

will have a chalky appearance in the thin layer over the glass. If it is too wet, it will wipe out of the cracks over your glass. If it is too dry it will be difficult to clean off the glass. Just keep an eye on it and maybe give it a test try. When the grout is dry enough, wipe it off the surface with a damp sponge or cloth. There will still be some streakiness coming from the cracks onto the surface of the glass. Let it dry some more and give it a final polish, piece by piece. It is exciting to watch the full effect of the color and luster emerge (Figure 2.39). Glue spots that accidently dried on top of the glass will become visible because the grout sticks to it. These spots can be easily scraped away with a razor blade. If you mixed your own grout and you intend to display your mosaic outdoors exposed to rain or snow, it is advisable to apply a grout sealant from the hardware store.

Never put leftover grout down the drain. Dispose anything with grout on it into the trash can.

Mindfulness and Art

Making art can have a strong positive impact on psychological health. As a practicing art therapist for many years, I have seen the power of art help transform many people's sense of well-being. Set an intention of enjoying the process and exploration of making art using stained glass mosaics as a method of self-care to calm and nurture yourself. The concept of zen can mean a state of calm, using direct, intuitive insights as a way of thinking or acting. Try to clear your mind of clutter and racing thoughts to become present in the moment without judgment. Observe what you are experiencing through your senses as you work. Does nipping glass release tension for you? Does piecing glass or spreading grout bring you calmness?

Approach your art without expectation. Notice your thoughts and feelings, whether negative or positive, but don't attempt to fix or react to them. Accept your thoughts, then let them go, bringing you back into the moment. For example, if you are piecing together glass and the shapes don't fit together the way you want them to, you may become frustrated with the irregular gaps between the glass. To shift that to a nonjudgmental thought you can simply observe the variation in the spaces and then let the thought go rather than trying to start over or correct what you perceive as a problem. Later when you grout your mosaic you may find your lines to be pleasing and more interesting than something more uniform. If you are still disappointed, try to let the thought go by focusing on the moment and accepting your learning process. Remember there is no right or wrong way to create your designs.

A personal example of coping with disappointment occurred when I was commissioned to create a large stained glass mosaic window for a new client. The client supplied me with an original window from his house that was more than a hundred years old. He liked my style and gave me artistic license to create whatever I wanted. It was an exciting opportunity to have free creative reign over the project and be paid to do it. I worked on the piece for months without too much of a preconceived plan, spontaneously choosing colors and shapes to build on a floral design. I grouted the window outside to witness the sunlight passing through each gem of color as I wiped the pieces clean. The finished mosaic looked beautiful. It was leaning against a deck rail when I walked about ten

Figure 2.40 The glass behind this piece is cracked, but it is still beautiful.

feet away to grout another window. Minutes later there was a loud bang. I knew what had happened before turning around to witness the window lying facedown on the deck. I froze where I was, allowing myself to take a few deep breaths and accepting the thought that whatever happened was now done and out of my control. When I walked over to assess the damage, I saw that the original window backing the stained glass was shattered into hundreds of pieces. The mosaic was still intact because of the strong adhesive quality of the glue and grout. However, because of the shattered backing, the window appeared cracked and was no longer structurally sound. I managed to take a few more deep breaths to remain calm and decide how to respond. I could potentially save the piece by pouring a clear resin over the back of the window to permanently hold it together. Although this would restore the structural integrity of the window, the cracks in the shattered glass would still show through. I decided I couldn't cope with moving forward on the project. My joy came from the process of creating and my promise to deliver an intact completed piece of art. I called my client to tell him what happened, offering him the damaged piece without accepting any payment. He could try to repair the piece or throw it in the trash. I was ready to let go of my disappointment and move on (Figure 2.40).

My client beamed when he first saw the mosaic. He thought it was beautiful and offered to pay me for it. I thanked him but declined the money. Several weeks later he called to tell me he had repaired the window and it was hanging in his house. He thought the cracks added character and he enjoyed the story behind them. He was so excited about the art that he commissioned me to make two more windows for him. Of course, I created these with extra care and again took pleasure in the process of my own creation. When I delivered the two additional windows to him, the check he gave me was already written to include the full amount of all three mosaics (Figure 2.41).

It was not in my control for this story to end happily. Before knowing the outcome, I had already achieved a sense of well-being knowing I enjoyed the process even if the product failed. Becoming emotionally reactive to my thoughts would not have solved the problem and would have made me feel worse. The same was true of my client. Practicing mindfulness can reduce impulsivity and increase compassion for ourselves and others.

By now you should be ready to choose a glass mosaic project and be excited about making art. Begin each creative session by quieting your body, emptying your mind, and allowing wellness in without judgment. Enjoy!

Figure 2.41 Three window mosaics

CHAPTER 3

QUILT PATTERN COASTERS AND TRIVETS

Figure 3.1 Quilt designs are great inspiration for mosaics, and a good place to start.
MAXCAB/ISTOCK VIA GETTY IMAGES

Figure 3.2 Glass tiles can be used to make mosaic coasters and trivets with no cutting involved.

Figure 3.3 Familiarity with the color wheel can help you choose colors that work well together, or you can trust your own color instincts.

Figure 3.4 The complementary pairs of blue/orange, yellow/purple, and red/green work well together.

The projects in this chapter are a great introduction to mosaics. They are very easy because there is no cutting involved. Almost anyone aged three to 103 can have success, including those with arthritis or muscle weakness in the hands. Your joy will come from exploring color and pattern based on ideas from traditional quilts using square vitreous tiles.

You can randomly explore color combinations or use ideas based on the color wheel (Figure 3.3).

Primary colors are yellow, blue, and red. Secondary colors are orange, green, and purple. Complementary colors are colors that are directly opposite on the color wheel: yellow and purple, orange and blue, red and green (Figure 3.4). Warm colors remind us of fire and heat: shades of yellow, orange, and red, while cool colors remind us of snow, ice, and dense forests: blues, purples, and greens.

When you want colors to look blended or homogenous, choose a palette of analogous

Figure 3.5 This quilt uses analogous colors in its design.

AILIME/ISTOCK VIA GETTY IMAGES

Figure 3.6 The use of complementary colors (red and green) makes this design pop. AILIME/ISTOCK VIA GETTY IMAGES

Figure 3.7 Contrast makes a bold design. OXYGEN/MOMENT VIA

GETTY IMAGES

Figure 3.8 Quilt with contrasting neutral tones by Robin Jones

Figure 3.9
In this block, neutral tones blend together for a calming effect.

colors, meaning close together on the color wheel (Figure 3.5).

To create patterns that pop out or contrast, use complimentary colors (Figure 3.6).

Contrast in value (lights and darks) will also create bolder designs (Figures 3.7 and 3.8).

Neutral tones such as black, white, tan, and gray can be found in warm or cool hues and can be placed accordingly for subtle or contrasting effects (Figures 3.8 and 3.9).

In quilt making, fabric shapes are sewn together to form a geometric whole, called a patchwork. Some patterns are created by making smaller patterns and repeatedly piecing them together to form blocks. The examples used to teach this project will be designed with either eight or nine squares across, depending on whether you are making a patchwork design with an even or odd number of squares. The dimensions of the surface and the tile sizes given will allow you to create patterns with appropriate size grout spaces. No measuring will be needed.

QUILT PATTERN COASTERS AND TRIVETS

INSTRUCTIONS

1. Prepare your surface. If you are cutting cement board into squares refer to instructions in Basic Techniques (pages 11–15). Otherwise, use a precut square from wood or other firm material according to coaster or trivet size.

2. Prepare the tiles. Some tiles come in sheets backed on paper or mesh. To remove paper backing, soak sheet in warm water for five to ten minutes until tiles slide easily off the paper. To remove tiles from mesh, peel them off. You can also glue a series of mesh tiles down by leaving the backing on if you are using multiple tiles of the same color next to each other. While working, keep tiles out on paper plates, sorted by color. Store easily in ziplock bags when finished.

3. Design. When creating designs using an odd number of tiles, arrange in rows of nine or work in blocks of nine squares, leaving even space between tiles so you can visualize your grout

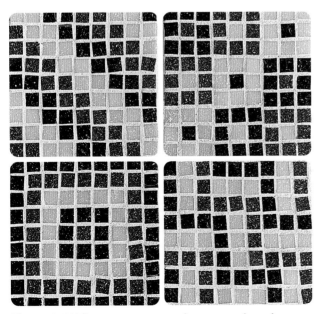

Figure 3.10 These coasters use the same color scheme but different designs.

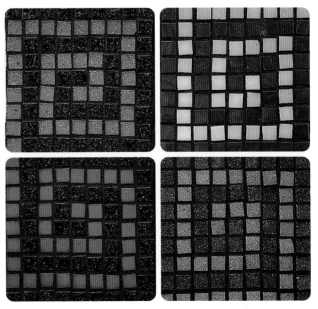

Figure 3.11 Here we have the same pattern but in different colors.

Figures 3.12, 3.13, and **3.14** One-of-a-kind coasters.

Figure 3.15 Design

Figure 3.16 Arrange

lines. Choose the smaller size surface for creating designs with an even number of tiles arranged in rows of eight, or with a repeated design of four blocks, sixteen tiles each. Make sure that all your tiles are the same thickness to create an even surface for placing drinks or serving dishes on your finished pieces. Play around with different combinations until you get a design that pleases you. Coasters usually come in sets of at least four, and multiple trivets may be placed on the table at the same time. Single squares can be placed together to form a larger design resembling blocks of a quilt. A set can be comprised of variations on a theme such as different designs using the same color scheme (Figure 3.10) or by repeating the same pattern using different colors (Figure 3.11).

Of course, you can make every square unique so each guest can choose a one-of-a-kind piece of art when using a coaster (Figures 3.12, 3.13, and 3.14).

If you like to create a plan or enjoy coloring patterns you can use graph paper and colored pencils to create ideas (Figure 3.15). I prefer to arrange and rearrange designs directly with the tiles. If you are working on cement board, the score lines can help you place the tiles evenly (Figure 3.16). You can continue to play around

Figures 3.17 and **3.18** Quilt by Robin Jones. I used the pattern from this quilt and similar colors to design this mosaic.

Figures 3.19 and **3.20** Quilt by Robin Jones. The center pattern of this quilt works well for a square mosaic design.

Figure 3.21 Here I used the traditional Nine Patch quilt design.

and make changes for as long as you like until you decide to glue. This is your first step to enjoying the process. See some examples of quilt designs made into mosaics in Figures 3.17, 3.18, 3.19, 3.20, and 3.21.

4. Glue the tiles. When you are happy with your design, it is time to glue down the tiles (Figure 3.22). For this project I recommend using tile adhesive in a tub. Your piece will be small enough that you can spread adhesive on the entire surface and have time to place the tiles before it dries. For this method, gently slide your tiles off the surface onto the table to maintain your pattern or have a spare surface ready to transfer the tiles onto. Take a plastic knife or any similar tool and spread the adhesive uniformly over the entire square. Place your tiles one at a time into the wet adhesive. If glue squishes up between grout lines, remove with a pointed stick. The adhesive dries fairly quickly, so if you would like to take your time or you are covering a larger surface use the "butter back" method. Simply spread adhesive on the back of the tiles one at a time as if you are buttering each tile. This is a

Figure 3.23 To glue all your tiles at once, lay wide tape across the top of all the tiles.

3.22 Glue

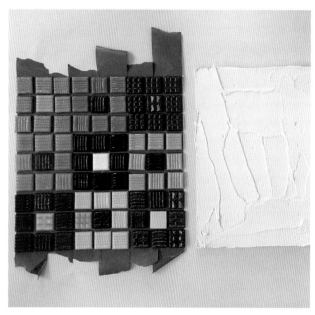

Figure 3.24 Spread adhesive to the size of your piece on the backing.

good method when using the three-quarter-inch tiles because they are easy to hold.

If you want to glue all the tiles at once, lay wide painters' or adhesive tape across all of the tiles (Figure 3.23). The tiles must be evenly spaced before taping. Pick up the taped sheet from your surface, spread the adhesive as described, and place the entire design onto the glue (Figures 3.24 and 3.25). When it is completely dry, remove the tape, and your design will remain intact (Figure 3.26).

Figure 3.25 Flip and place your design onto the glue.

3.27 Clean up excess adhesive.

5. Grout (Figure 3.28). Everything you need to know about grouting is in the Basic Techniques section (pages 11–15) in Chapter 2. Scale back the quantity to mix a small amount of grout. I started with a half a cup of water and added approximately one and a half cups of grout. This was enough to cover eight coasters and two trivets.

Figure 3.26 When the adhesive is dry, remove the tape.

3.28 Grout

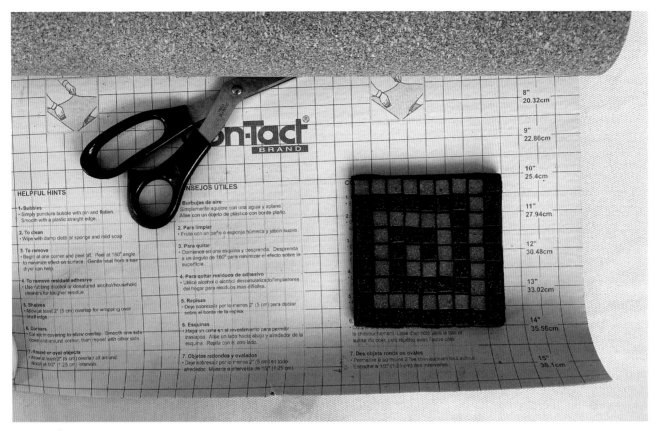

3.29 Cork

6. Add finishing touches. Use grout sealer to prevent food and drink stains. To protect your furniture and have a functional piece of art, use self-adhesive cork sheets or tabs on the bottom of your work. Coasters have a nice feel and look to them if you cover the entire bottom with cork (Figure 3.29). This product comes in a roll from the hardware store and can be cut into any size or shape. Using small tabs or circles can be an alternative to covering the bottom of your piece. If you choose this option, you can paint the bottom of your piece to match or contrast with the grout. Acrylic craft paint comes in hundreds of colors and is available at craft stores for about a dollar a bottle. If you already have paints, almost any kind will work.

3.30 Finished coaster

Challenges and Variations

Try varying the size of the base and your tiles to create a whole new series of patterns (Figures 3.31 and 3.32). Use rectangular shapes in combination with squares. If the piece does not have to be functional you can experiment with varying thicknesses of tiles. Consider making an art piece for your wall. You can work with a larger surface area or create a wall arrangement with multiple smaller squares. If using multiple small squares, you can hang them with or without space between them using picture frame hooks attached to the squares with construction adhesive. Hang the squares in a permanent arrangement or rearrange them to form new patterns when the mood strikes. Coaster-size squares can be kept on a coffee table for you and your guests to slide around into new patterns while relaxing.

By skipping ahead in the book, you can use the techniques in the chapter on trays and tables to create more complicated quilt patterns by cutting sheet glass (Figure 3.33).

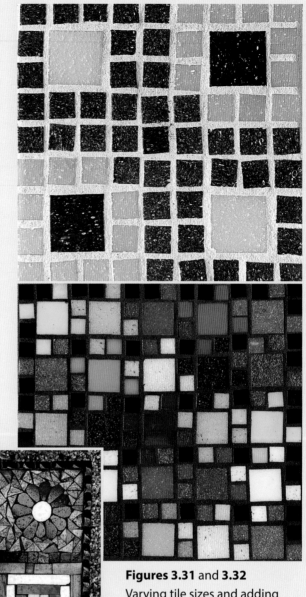

Figures 3.31 and **3.32** Varying tile sizes and adding contrast move the eye around and make these pieces interesting.

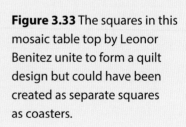

Figure 3.33 The squares in this mosaic table top by Leonor Benitez unite to form a quilt design but could have been created as separate squares as coasters.

CHAPTER 4

TRAYS AND TABLES

◇◇◇◇◇◇◇◇◇◇◇◇◇◇◇◇◇◇◇◇◇

Making mosaic trays and tables can provide easy or challenging choices to create functional art, depending on the size and complexity of your design. The easiest option would be to follow the instructions for the quilt pattern project on a square or rectangular ready-made tray or small table (Figures 4.1 and 4.2). If you are ready to start nipping and cutting glass, you will have infinite possibilities to explore shapes, color, and composition to create a mosaic. Different approaches and subject matter allow you to choose the process best suited for you. The common feature of this project series is working on flat surfaces mostly with opaque glass.

Butterfly tray by Leonor Benitez

Figure 4.1 It's easy to upgrade an existing square or rectangular tray with tiles. Tiled tray by Meredith Ormsby.

Figure 4.2 Attach square tiles to a table for a whole new look.

TRAYS AND TABLES

MATERIALS

- For the tray surface choose any shape ready-made tray with a smooth, rigid surface (Figure 4.3). You can make over an old tray from your house or a yard sale or buy a new tray. Inexpensive trays are available at department and craft stores such as Ikea, Target, or Michaels.
- For the table surface use a table instead of a tray. Work directly on the table or create a new tabletop by cutting cement board to size and placing it directly over an old or marred tabletop.
- For the glass select a variety of sheet glass or tiles of the same thickness.
- When choosing your adhesive consider your other material. If you use glass sheets with any transparency and you do not want the color of the tray to show through, choose a white adhesive and/or paint the surface white before you begin. Read the package directions to be sure the adhesive will work with the material of your tray.

Figure 4.3 Any shape tray can be embellished with glass tiles.

Figure 4.4 Buddhist sandpainting mandala sand art in Lhasa, Tibet

LORENTRAGER/ISTOCK/GETTY IMAGES PLUS VIA GETTY IMAGES

Mandala Tray

The word *mandala* is Sanskrit for "circle." Mandalas have their origin in eastern spiritual traditions. A circle is a shape representing wholeness and unity with no beginning or end. Mandala is a universal form in nature found in planets, flowers, shells, and snowflakes. The creation of mandalas can be used as a stress release through art therapy, adult coloring pages, meditation, or mosaic art. Making a mosaic mandala will allow you to feel focused and grounded while you work spontaneously in a playful, accepting manner. You will create a unique design by repeating glass shapes and colors radiating from the center.

INSTRUCTIONS

1. Choose a round tray for your surface. This example is a fifteen-inch, brass-plated tray from Ikea (Figure 4.5).

Figure 4.5 Brass-plated tray from Ikea

2. Glass scraps work great for this project. Find or cut a center shape or a series of similar shapes. Begin by placing the shapes radiating out from the center (Figures 4.6 and 4.7). There is no need to make them perfectly symmetric. Your design will develop a balanced organic appearance, much like flowers or animal forms. I started my

Figures 4.6 and **4.7** Begin placing glass from the center outward.

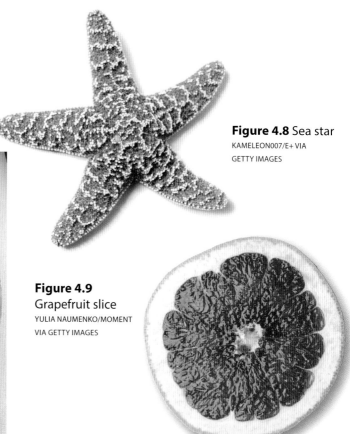

Figure 4.8 Sea star
KAMELEON007/E+ VIA GETTY IMAGES

Figure 4.9 Grapefruit slice
YULIA NAUMENKO/MOMENT VIA GETTY IMAGES

arrangement on a paper plate. Once I settled on a center design, I began gluing the pieces to the tray. It is a good idea to start gluing before you have too many small loose pieces. Notice the influence of the sea star, grapefruit, and ferns in the center design (Figures 4.8, 4.9, and 4.10).

Figure 4.10 Fern center GEORGECLERK/E+ VIA GETTY IMAGES

Figure 4.11 Yellow triangles were used for one circle.

Figure 4.12 Measure before gluing to be sure your design is centered.

Figures 4.13 and **4.14** The pink petal shapes are similar to the outer petals of a rose.

3. Build out from your center. I found one yellow triangle scrap and decided to repeat the shape. I used a glass cutter to form similar triangles without measuring (Figure 4.11). By this time, I had a rhythm going and was absorbed in the process.

4. Fill in background spaces by nipping and piecing glass. Before I glued the yellow and purple pieces, I measured the distance of each yellow point to the edge of the tray to make sure my design was remaining centered (Figure 4.12). I had to adjust the position of a few of the points so the remaining space was about the same all the way around.

5. Keep building on your design. Next I added a ring of three-eighth-inch glass tiles and then pink petal shapes. Notice the shape and sizes of the petals vary like the outer petals of a rose (Figures 4.13 and 4.14).

6. Add designs until your tray is completely filled. Continue to nip and cut glass to fit. Consider whether you want to repeat shapes and colors or continue making new designs. With little space remaining I began working from the pink petals outward, and from the edge inward, to complete my design. I repeated the triangular shapes and the orange color I used earlier. Blue was introduced as a new color (Figures 4.15 and 4.16). I chose it because it is the complement of orange. It helped the edge to show up well and frame the design.

7. Grout and seal according to directions (Figure 4.17).

Figures 4.15 and **4.16** Pieces of blue glass complement the orange and fill out the design.

Figure 4.17 The completed mandala tray

Challenges and Variations

There are so many ways to play with the circular shape! Creating a symmetric mandala can offer a challenge or fulfill a need if you want more structure. Measure and draw out a pattern directly on the tray or table and nip and cut your glass to fit the shapes.

Figures 4.18 and **4.19**
Mandala tables by
Leonor Benitez

4.20 Mandala tray by Meredith Ormsby

Figure 4.21
Try making a mandala within a square, as in this table by Leonor Benitez.

FLAMING PUMPKIN/E+
VIA GETTY IMAGES

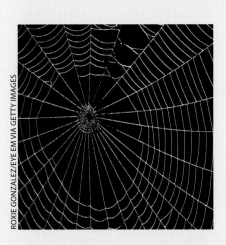

Figures 4.22, 4.23, and **4.24**
Notice how this mandala by Leonor Benitez is asymmetric like a nautilus shell or spider web.

Tray or Table as Inspiration

If you find a tray or table that already has an interesting design to it, you can use the design or images as inspiration for your mosaic. For instance, Leonor Benitez found a table that had flowers in the ironwork below the tabletop (Figure 4.25). She repeated the design by using the same shape flowers in her mosaic. Notice the way the colorful flowers tie together with the iron flowers below. The black grout creates a repetition of the line pattern.

Choose a tray or table that already has a design on it that won't be covered by the mosaic. I chose this tray from Ikea because of the delightful little pattern of birds and leaves around the edges (Figure 4.26). The long beaks on the birds in this design inspired me to use hummingbirds.

Figure 4.25 Flower mosaic table by Leonor Benitez

INSTRUCTIONS

1. Draw your design directly on the mosaic surface. I used photos as a reference to sketch the birds in pencil (Figure 4.27).

2. Choose colors that appeal to you, then nip and cut sheet glass pieces to fill in the pencil lines. The placement of the birds was important to me, so I made them first and glued them down (Figure 4.28).

Figure 4.26 The birds and leaves in the edge design of this tray are my inspiration.

Figure 4.27 Hummingbirds drawn on in pencil

Figure 4.28 Make your main motifs first, and glue them down.

3. After you have the focus of your piece completed, either draw or directly arrange the other images (Figure 4.29). I cut a bunch of small leaf pieces from different shades of green glass. I didn't draw the leaves on the tray because I wanted to play around with the placement until I was satisfied. I arranged these around the birds and glued them down.

4. Fill in the tray completely. If you save the background for last, it is easy to piece around the glued images. I used two shades of blue three-quarter-inch tiles for the background to provide some variation in the color (Figure 4.30). By using tiles, I was starting with small pieces that would be easy to nip and fill in around the birds and leaves.

5. Grout and seal the piece (Figure 4.31).

Figure 4.29 Leaves are added next, without drawing them first.

Figure 4.30 The background is filled in with two shades of blue glass.

Figure 4.31 The completed hummingbird tray

Animal Trays and Tables

Animals are fun and interesting images to use on mosaics. Fish, reptiles, birds, and amphibians are easy to draw and have so many varied textures, patterns, and colors. I've chosen a lizard to demonstrate for a tray because the form fits well on the rectangular shape. Follow the instructions to create your own lizard or any animal of your choice.

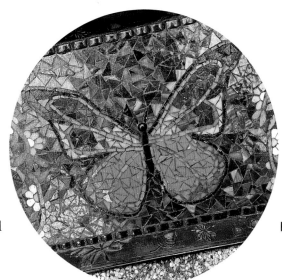

Figure 4.32 Nearly any animal or insect can be the inspiration for a mosaic. Some will be more challenging than others. This butterfly tray by Leonor Benitez has a lot of variations in color and shapes.

INSTRUCTIONS

1. Select a tray or table. Choose an animal that will fit well given the proportion of the surface. Use animal photos to get ideas and to sketch from (Figure 4.33). Make some practice drawings or sketch out the animal directly on the tray.

2. Decide if you want to use non-representational or realistic colors and select your glass (Figure 4.34). Remember to be sure the glass is all the same thickness so the tray surface is even and functional. The glass beads, tiles, and sheet glass used for the lizard worked well together to create an even surface. Try out different combinations of glass to begin filling in your animal (Figure 4.35).

Figure 4.33 Find an image of your subject to help you draw it accurately. This is a gecko commonly known as the Thai bow-fingered gecko. ARUN ROISRI/MOMENT VIA GETTY IMAGES

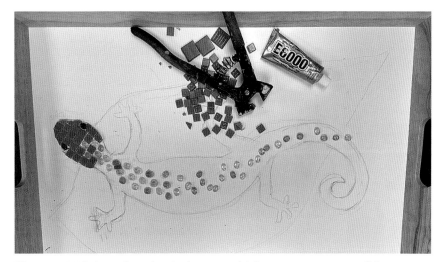

Figure 4.34 Select glass that is the same thickness so your tray will be even and functional.

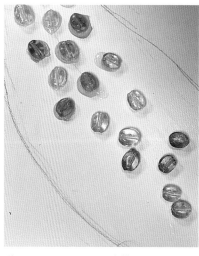

Figure 4.35 Try out different placements of the glass, and glue when you are satisfied.

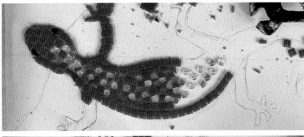

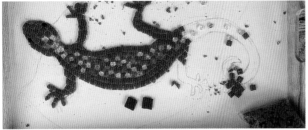

Figures 4.36 and **4.37** Continue adding and gluing pieces for your main motif.

Figures 4.38 and **4.39** I used sheet glass and varied greens to bring a different dimension to the leaf.

3. Continue piecing and gluing (Figures 4.36 and 4.37).

4. Think about other elements to add to the design. I used sheet glass for the leaf to contrast the variation in tone with the flat color tiles in the background (Figures 4.38 and 4.39). The fly was added as an afterthought when I was finishing up the background (Figure 4.40).

5. Grout and seal to finish the mosaic (Figure 4.41).

Figure 4.40 I added the fly as I was finishing up the background.

Figure 4.41 The completed tray

Challenges and Variations

Try a mammal or sea creature for a more challenging form. Choose from safari animals, farm animals, or your own pets. Animals with prints such as tigers, zebras, giraffes, and turtles provide interesting options. For a major ongoing project, attempt a large animal table. For my first glass mosaic I had a memorable experience of making a three-foot diameter tabletop to cover a tree stump next to my house. The stump was visible directly outside my kitchen door but could not be removed. I thought the only solution was to turn it into art. I had a contractor saw a circular base out of a sheet of cement board that was then bolted to the stump in a level position. Since the mosaic process was new to me, I looked at the project as a learning opportunity without expectation of the finished product. I already disliked the unsightly stump, so I figured anything I made would be an improvement. It was summer, so I could work outside on location at my leisure. I didn't have to worry about taking up space in my house or leaving a mess around. I chose an octopus for its simple form that allowed for variation in the positioning of the tentacles (Figure 4.42). I drew my design directly on the cement board and made my first trip to a local mosaic store to buy tiles and pick up some free advice.

My daughter had just graduated college and was spending her last summer at home before permanently moving away to start her new life in the fall. With free time on her hands, she joined me for hours of piecing and gluing the mosaic. We worked together quietly or with casual conversation in a process that let us absorb the emotions of our changing relationship. The finished product was more beautiful than I would have anticipated, but the process was the most important part of the project. After several years the table was damaged and eventually destroyed by severe weather (mostly ice and snow), but my memory of the experience will last a lifetime. If you make mosaics for exposed areas outside, make sure you can protect them or bring them inside for the winter.

Figure 4.42 Completed octopus mosaic on tree stump.

Artist-Inspired Trays and Tables

Many artists throughout history have influenced and copied each other's work. If you find yourself at a loss for ideas, or you simply need a little help with color and composition, try copying from one of the masters. There are countless artists from the twentieth century who painted bold simple designs that can be easily translated into mosaic pieces. Consider works by Andy Warhol, Piet Mondrian (Figure 4.43), Amedeo Modigliani, and Paul Klee to name a few. Aboriginal dot paintings also lend well to mosaic designs (Figures 4.44).

Figure 4.43
Abstract modern painting in Mondrian style, seamless pattern

MYSONDANUBE/DIGITALVISION-
VECTORS VIA GETTY IMAGES

Figure 4.44
Aboriginal painting in Kundjarra granite boulders, Northern Territory, Australia

WESTEND61/WESTEND61 VIA GETTY IMAGES

Figure 4.45 Reworking of *Messenger of Autumn* by Paul Klee THEMAGICMANDALAMAKER/ALAMY STOCK PHOTO

INSTRUCTIONS

1. Search for a painting you would like to use for a tray or table. I like *Messenger of Autumn* by Paul Klee (Figure 4.45) because of the balance of the composition and the simplicity of the design. The tray table I used has a wide gray edge that matched well with the color scheme.

2. Sketch out the basic shapes in the painting on the mosaic surface or paper. I did my drawing on paper. Since the shapes were easy, all I had to do on the tray was mark how wide the columns of rectangles were to get the proper proportion (Figure 4.46).

3. Choose the glass you would like to use. I used both tiles and sheet glass to get a variety of subtle colors. Notice how using tiles created additional line patterns in the design.

Figure 4.46 Sketch out the basic shapes of your design.

4. Begin cutting and piecing the glass. I started with the tree. It is the focal point of the piece and I wanted it placed just right. I glued the tree down as soon as I got the shape and then continued to glue as I worked (Figure 4.47). Start gluing whenever you feel comfortable.

Figure 4.47 I started by placing and gluing the glass for the tree.

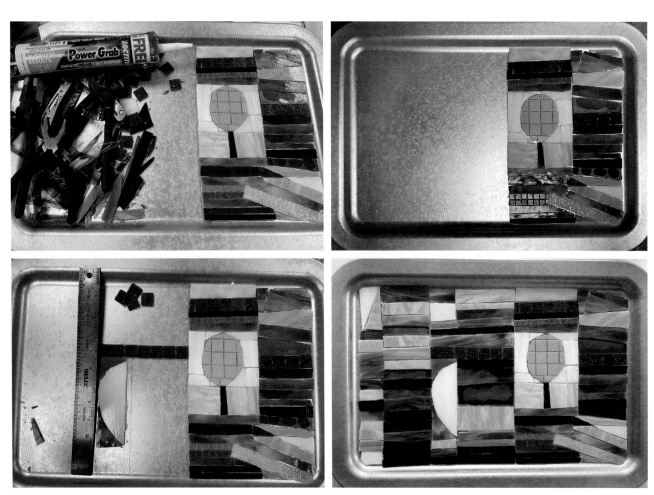

Figures 4.48, 4.49, 4.50, and **4.51** Placing the pieces from right to left

5. After completing the section with the tree, I worked mainly from right to left except when I was placing the second round piece. Most of the cuts were straight, so it was easy to work along at a good pace without too much stopping and thinking (Figures 4.48, 4.49, 4.50, 4.51).

6. Grout and seal the mosaic. This tray detaches from its base so it can be used as a tray or a table (Figures 4.52 and 4.53).

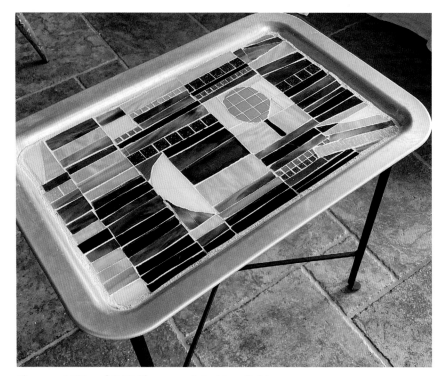

Figures 4.52 and **4.53** The completed tray/table

Challenges and Variations

The artist Henri Matisse is famous for his use of bright colors and patterns in his paintings. Matisse is also known for his cut-out collages made from his hand-painted papers and his stained glass windows (Figure 4.54). My favorite of Matisse's cutouts is called *Icarus* (Figure 4.55). It has personal meaning and I wanted to copy it as a design for an outdoor coffee table. I made it out of tiles glued to cement board (Figure 4.56). Find an art piece that has meaning for you and create a large mosaic version of that painting. Decide how you might want to personalize it by changing the colors or adding your own images. For a real challenge try translating something more realistic like *The Mona Lisa*!

Figure 4.54 Stained glass windows for a chapel made from cut out paper design of Matisse, Henri Matisse in Nice, Alpes Maritimes, South France

AGEFOTOSTOCK/ALAMY STOCK PHOTO

Figure 4.55 *Icarus* is a paper cutout by Henri Matisse (1869–1954) in 1945 from his book *Jazz,* which was published in 1947 by Teriade.

DENNIS HALLINAN/ALAMY STOCK PHOTO

Figure 4.56 My version of *Icarus.*

CHAPTER 5

TRANSPARENT GLASS

Creating with transparent glass adds the element of light to your work. In addition to considering shape, color, line, and texture, there is now the beauty of light passing through your art. As you work on the projects in this section play around with the glass by holding different colors up to light. Observe how varying amounts of transparency allow the light to pass through and how it is projected on other surfaces. If transparent glass is placed in a window, the colors and projections will change throughout the day. Depending on the project, light sources can vary between sunlight, candles, and electric lights. The images in Figures 5.1, 5.2, 5.3, 5.4, and 5.5 are of stained glass windows projected on a white canvas from sunlight through a window. They look like paintings in and of themselves.

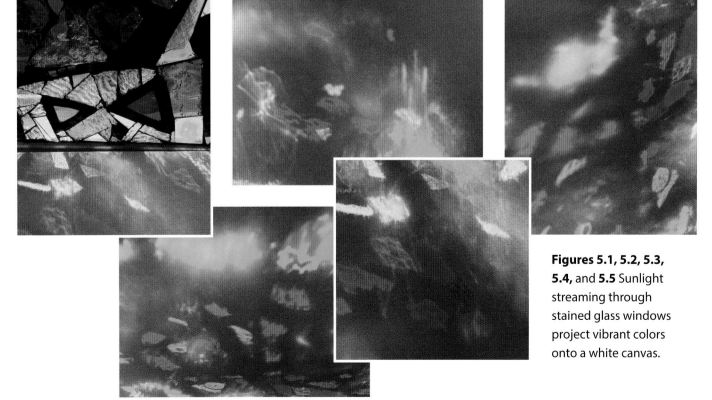

Figures 5.1, 5.2, 5.3, 5.4, and **5.5** Sunlight streaming through stained glass windows project vibrant colors onto a white canvas.

SMALL PICTURE FRAME WINDOW

An easy way to begin working with transparent glass is on a small, flat surface such as a picture frame. An eight- by ten-inch frame will give you enough space for your glass pieces to be of a manageable size, but not so big that the project will feel overwhelming for a beginner.

MATERIALS
- 8 x 10-inch picture frame and glass with backing removed
- Small transparent pieces of colored glass
- Clear adhesive
- Grout (optional)
- Screw eyes or small hooks to hang frame in a window

INSTRUCTIONS

1. Prepare a small picture frame by removing backing and gluing the glass into the frame to create a framed windowpane.

2. Choose your subject matter. A tree will be used as the example for this project. You can select any simple image or design or copy the tree.

3. Draw your subject. There is one simple rule to drawing a natural-looking tree. The widest part of a tree is at the base of the trunk. Each time a tree branches out it will be narrower in diameter than the branch it is growing from. If the forms continue to get narrower as they grow, the tree will look natural. I recommend keeping the tree simple (Figure 5.7). An easy way to create branches is to draw a V where you would like to place a branch. Add Vs to attach smaller and smaller branches. Another way to add branches is to draw a trunk and add on smaller branches the higher up you go. The easiest option is to draw a trunk with dense enough foliage to cover the branches.

Figure 5.6 Any small picture frame can be used as a base for a stained glass project. Remove the backing and glue the glass into the frame.

Figure 5.7 Examples of simple tree drawings

4. Begin with a drawing placed under the glass to size or build your tree without a drawing by piecing glass bits to form a trunk and branches.

5. Choose glass colors (Figure 5.8). A flowering or imaginary tree will provide endless possibilities. This is a good project for using up scraps.

6. Fill in your design by nipping and cutting glass according to the directions in the Materials and Techniques chapter. Nip and place glass pieces starting at the base of the trunk. Work up the tree forming branches if you want them.

7. Fill in the foliage with small scraps of glass (Figure 5.9). Nip to fit. It is okay to leave space for the sky or background to show through. Every tree is different, so there is no right or wrong way to place the bits of glass. Try to achieve a balanced look through shape and color.

8. Glue down tree pieces.

9. Cut and glue background pieces. To balance the colors, I chose bits of pink on a green ground, which is the opposite of the pink flowering tree with bits of green leaves. To give the illusion of nature in the background, I used a unique piece of clear glass that was flecked and streaked with shades of green (Figure 5.10).

10. Optional grout. I wanted to maintain the light, airy feeling of this piece without lines breaking up the composition, so I decided not to grout it.

11. Use lightweight picture-hanging hardware to hang the finished piece in a window or lean it on a sill.

Figure 5.8 The glass colors I chose for my tree

Figure 5.10 The completed tree picture

Figure 5.9
Tree with foliage added

LARGE PICTURE FRAME WINDOW

Using a large picture frame will give you the opportunity to explore any subject matter on an undivided sheet of glass. You can use one of the ideas from an earlier chapter of this book, such as quilt patterns, mandala, animal, or artist inspiration. For a different idea, look for photo references to choose any subject matter, including land or seascapes, a closeup of a tree or flower, or an abstract portrait. I recommend starting a picture file either digitally or in a paper folder with a collection of magazine clippings, your own photos, sketches, and examples of artwork you appreciate. Any time you see an image you find interesting, save it and use it later as inspiration. When I was searching for an artist's painting to use in the Trays and Tables chapter, I used a Paul Klee painting for a tray design but also came across another one of Klee's paintings called *Heroic Roses* that I thought would be perfect for this project (Figure 5.11). I fell in love with the composition, colors, and shapes in this painting. The heavy black outlines provide a good way to break up the large space. Feel free to copy this Paul Klee painting or choose any idea of your own.

Figure 5.11 *Heroic Roses,* 1938, by Paul Klee (1879–1940)

© FINE ART IMAGES/HERITAGE IMAGES VIA HERITAGE IMAGE PARTNERSHIP LTD/AMAMY STOCK PHOTO

INSTRUCTIONS

1. Select a large picture frame. This example is a twenty-six- by twenty-two-inch metal frame. The frame can be metal, wood, or a composite material. Keep it simple unless the frame is going to be incorporated into the design of the piece. Buying a new frame can be expensive, so I repurposed a frame from an old piece of art that I no longer had hanging on the wall. Garage sales are an excellent place to pick up old frames.

2. Replace thin glass with thicker windowpane glass cut to size from a hardware store or pour a layer of clear epoxy resin on the back of the glass to reinforce it. When I first started this project, I was worried the glass might be too thin to support the weight of the stained glass, but I started the project anyway. I hadn't gotten very far when the weight of the glued glass caused the

> **MATERIALS**
> - Large picture frame, at least 16 x 20 inches
> - Thick windowpane glass to fit frame and clear epoxy resin to reinforce strength of glass
> - Colored transparent glass in sheets or pieces. Glass may be of varying textures and thicknesses.
> - Small transparent or opaque glass tiles or pebbles (optional)
> - Clear adhesive
> - Black grout
> - Screw eyes or hooks to hang window

picture frame glass to crack. Rather than start over I reinforced the back with clear epoxy resin. I had never used a product like this before, but I tried it and my problem was solved. I looked online for a self-leveling, non-yellowing, two-part epoxy resin. The brand I chose is called ProMarine Supplies. I was very satisfied with the result and how easy the product was to

Figure 5.12 My sketch of *Heroic Roses*

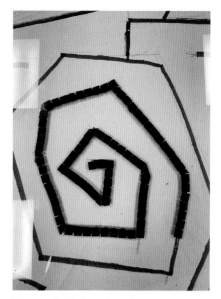

Figure 5.13 Starting the black outlines

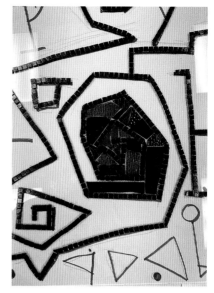

Figure 5.14 Nip and cut your glass and begin to fill in the design.

use. Apply it before your glass cracks. I am excited to explore this product for other artistic purposes in the future. If you don't want the expense or the mess, get a piece of thicker glass, but epoxy resin is the sturdier option.

3. Sketch out your idea on a piece of paper the size of your glass (Figure 5.12). Lay the frame over the drawing and you can follow your design by seeing it through the glass.

4. If your design has any thick black outlines, use three-eighth-inch black tiles to form the outline (Figure 5.13). Glue in place with clear adhesive. Make sure it sticks to nonporous surfaces.

5. Fill in your design by nipping and cutting glass according to the directions in the Materials and Techniques chapter (Figure 5.14). Since you can see through the glass it is easy to overlay and then trace any lines you may want to follow from the drawing below for the shape you want to fill

Figures 5.15 and **5.16** It is easy to see through the glass to trace your shapes with a Sharpie marker.

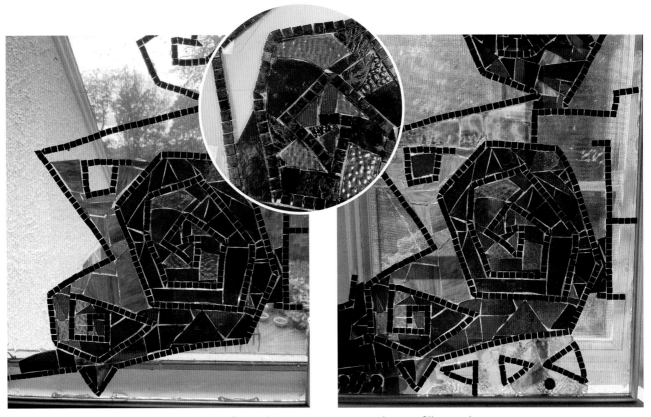

Figures 5.17, 5.18, 5.19 Continue to cut, fill, and glue your pieces in place to fill your shapes.

(Figures 5.15 and 5.16). Use a Sharpie marker. The lines can be easily removed with hand sanitizer or alcohol.

6. Glue all pieces in place. Avoid using Weld Bond brand adhesive for clear glass projects. I tried this product for the first time on this piece. It is easy to use (consistency of Elmer's glue), cleans up with soap and water, and is a strong adhesive that bonds almost everything. But after I finished the window, the adhesive was not turning clear (Figures 5.20 and 5.21). I researched the product and found that it needs air to cure clear. I had laid the glue on thick, and air could not get into the nonporous surfaces between the glass. Heat and ultraviolet light did eventually cure it, but it took months of sitting in sunlight. This is a great adhesive for opaque pieces, but not for this project.

7. Grout and display frame in window (Figure 5.22).

Figure 5.20 Front of piece before glue cleared

Figure 5.21 Back of piece before glue cleared

Challenges and Variations

Unlike making a tray, a picture frame window does not require an even surface. You can experiment with different thicknesses of glass and embellishments such as beads, marbles, pebbles, and small found glass objects.

Experiment with small pieces of opaque glass but remember light will not pass through. Choose a wide flat picture frame and paint a design or glue tiles to the frame to expand upon your art.

Figure 5.22 The completed picture

CYLINDRICAL LANTERN

By working on a cylinder, you can experience gluing glass to a curved surface. A cylinder is an easy way to start because it only curves in one direction. The lantern shown here has a repetitive pattern that doesn't require much skill or planning but yields a beautiful result. I chose this project to cope mentally and physically while experiencing a breakthrough case of COVID-19. I needed a distraction from my symptoms and isolation and found this lantern project to be very therapeutic.

INSTRUCTIONS

1. Select a glass cylinder (Figure 5.23). If you don't have one at home to repurpose, cylinders are available for just a few dollars at craft and home good stores.

2. Choose a color scheme for your glass (Figure 5.24). I had a partial sheet of bright orange that I wanted to start with. My goal was to make the pieces visually pop. Orange is a warm color. To make it stand out I surrounded it with its complementary color, blue, and other cool colors. I already had a tray full of cool colored scraps I could cut into rectangles.

MATERIALS
- A glass cylinder. The size used in this project is 6 inches high with a 5½-inch diameter. Any size will do, but make sure it is a cylinder and does not have a bottle neck or bulges. The cylinder lends well to using rectangular pieces of glass.
- Transparent, colored glass rectangles of various sizes
- Fast drying clear adhesive. I used Loctite Power Grab interior/exterior construction adhesive, available in hardware stores in the caulk section. It is described on the tube as "one second instant grab." This is important for a vertical or curved project so that the glass does not slip. This adhesive sticks instantly but still gives you plenty of wiggle room time before it cures.
- Grout
- Candle or battery-operated string lights

3. Use a glass cutter to cut strips of glass in various widths. Nip or cut glass to appropriate lengths as you go.

4. If you have a color that will stand out among the others, glue those pieces on first. I glued the orange pieces first in vertical positions spaced out around the cylinder (Figure 5.25).

Figure 5.23 Select a cylinder without many curves or bulges.

Figure 5.24 Choose your color scheme and select your glass.

Figure 5.25 Orange pieces glued in place

5. Fill in the rest of the cylinder with vertical rows of various thicknesses until the surface is filled (Figure 5.26). Stagger the lengths of the pieces so the horizontal cracks appear random. You do not need to measure. Fill in the pieces like a jigsaw puzzle and give a little nip to adjust the size when needed. If your pieces in each column are not evenly cut, the grout lines will have a beautiful variation.

6. Grout or leave the spaces empty to allow light through (Figures 5.27 and 5.28). I decided to use white grout to contrast with the dark colored glass. Since I made this piece when I wasn't feeling well, my craftsmanship was not up to par. The grout hid the rough edges of the glass and the glue that squished out into the cracks between the pieces.

7. Light your lantern with a candle or battery-operated string lights (Figures 5.29 and 5.30). This easy-to-make lantern will light up your life when you are feeling down!

Figure 5.26 Fill in the rest of the pieces around the cylinder.

Figure 5.27 Before grout is applied

Figure 5.28 The grouted cylinder

Figure 5.29
Left ungrouted, light will shine through the cracks between the glass pieces.

Figure 5.30
When grouted, the cracks will be dark areas when the piece is lit.

Challenges and Variations

Consider holiday-themed colors and shapes. Start with randomly placed glass pebbles instead of rectangles and work a design around them as Meredith Ormsby did in the radiating flowers in Figure 5.31.

Different styles of square lanterns provide flat surfaces to work on with four separate panels to create variations on a theme. Some lanterns are metal with glass inserts allowing for four distinct framed glass panels as in the lantern by Lenore Trujillo in Figures 5.32 and 5.33. Others are square glass vessels such as the containers with flower designs in Figures 5.34, 5.35, and 5.36, or the abstract design featuring warm versus cool colors in Figure 5.37. The two square vases by Dan Patrell in Figures 5.38 and 5.39 have Morse code messages encrypted in the designs.

Figure 5.31
Meredith Ormsby's flowered cylinder

Figures 5.32 and **5.33** Lantern by Lenore Trujillo

Figures 5.34, 5.35, and **5.36** Floral designs by Meredith Ormsby

Experiment with different shaped vessels (Figures 5.40 and 5.41). Use smaller pieces of glass to follow curved surfaces. Glass containers of any shape can be used as vases or lanterns. You can use narrow-necked vessels such as wine bottles that can be illuminated with wine cork battery operated string lights. If using your art as a vase, be sure to place it in a well-lit area to allow the light to pass through. Choose flowers to complement the color scheme of your glass.

Figure 5.37 Abstract warm/cool design by Meredith Ormsby

Figures 5.38 and **5.39** Dan Patrell encrypted messages in Morse code in these designs.

Figures 5.40 and **5.41** This vessel has completely different looks when used as a lantern vs. as a vase.

CHAPTER 6

MOSAIC MINIATURES

◇◇◇◇◇◇◇◇◇◇◇◇◇◇◇◇◇

Size is an important element to consider when making mosaics for both practical and aesthetic reasons. You may not have the space to work on large windows or to store or display finished works of art. Some people naturally like to work small when they make crafts and working large may be overwhelming. Small pieces demand focus from both the artist and the viewer. For the artist this focus can provide discipline and mental clarity. For the viewer miniature pieces have the power to draw one in closer, creating an intimate encounter with the piece. In order to explore this concept, all the projects in this chapter will be three inches or smaller. Use tweezers to place glass pieces if they are too small for your hands.

MINIATURE LIGHT CATCHERS AND PAPERWEIGHTS

Small glass picture frames or coasters, such as those in Figure 6.1, can be inexpensively purchased at craft and home goods stores. With only three easy steps, anyone can create an imaginative light catcher or paperweight in one sitting.

MATERIALS
- Small glass picture frame or coaster, 3 inches or smaller
- Small scraps of transparent glass, beads, and other embellishments
- Two-part clear epoxy resin

INSTRUCTIONS

1. Gather your materials. This is a great project for using up small glass scraps and shards left over from other projects (Figure 6.2).

2. Arrange small pieces in the recessed area of the picture frame or coaster (Figure 6.3). Simply piece scraps together as you would a jigsaw puzzle. Unless you plan to use this as a coaster, glass pieces and beads can vary in thickness. Colors and shapes will appear random. No cutting is necessary unless you want to fit a particular color in a certain space.

3. Mix a very small amount of two-part, self-settling clear epoxy resin. Pour over glass design and allow to cure. The resin will hold the glass in place. No gluing or grouting. Display flat or in a window when dry (Figures 6.4 and 6.5).

Figure 6.1 Start with inexpensive glass picture frames or coasters.

Figure 6.2 You will only need a small amount of glass for miniatures, so this is a great time to use up leftover pieces.

Figure 6.3 Arrange glass until you are happy with the placement.

Figures 6.4 and **6.5** Pour two-part epoxy resin over the glass and allow to cure. Your miniatures are finished and ready to display.

TEA LIGHT CANDLE VOTIVES

This project is more challenging than the light catcher or paperweight because it involves gluing small pieces of glass around a tightly curved candle holder. However, because of the size of the piece, this project does not take a long time to complete. You can enjoy making one or sets of several to display at home or give as gifts.

INSTRUCTIONS FOR TEALIGHT VOTIVE #1

1. Gather your materials. For the first example, you will need strings of threaded glass beads. It is much easier to glue strings of beads rather than individual beads, especially if you want to form lines.

2. Use a clear adhesive that is thick and dries quickly so beads won't slip as you rotate the votive. Draw a line of glue directly on the votive and place the beads in the glue. Thicker adhesives will typically have a tube opening much wider than the beads. To draw a thin line, squeeze a dab of glue onto another surface and use a pointy object such as a nail to dip into the glue and spread it in a line on the votive. You may have to do this a small segment at a time to press the beads in place and work your way around the glass (Figures 6.7 and 6.8). Allow extra thread at

the ends of the strand so the beads won't slip off as you are working. You can trim the extra thread when the glue dries. I chose a curvy line to create a sense of fluidity. It is also easier than trying to create a straight line. Make whatever kinds of lines you would like. You can opt for straight, curvy, zigzag, vertical, horizontal, or spirals.

3. I added a second curvy line using a different type of bead (Figure 6.9). These lines will become borders between the areas of colored glass. Let the glue dry before trying to fit other pieces of glass into your design. The dry beaded lines will support other pieces of glass so they don't slip.

4. Choose a single larger bead or glass embellishment if you want a focal point in your design. I used an amber glass pebble.

Figure 6.6 Start with a glass votive candle holder approximately two inches high by two inches in diameter.

Figures 6.7 and **6.8** Draw a line of quick-drying glue and attach your string of beads onto the glue.

Figure 6.9 Another string of beads was added here. Once the glue is dry, these lines of beads will help to support the other glass pieces you will add.

Figure 6.10 The amber focal point has been added. Primary colors will fill in the rest of the design.

5. After I glued the amber piece in place, I sorted through glass scraps to choose the rest of my colors. You can do this before you start. I like to decide as I go. I ultimately settled on using primary colors to fill in the remaining areas (Figure 6.10).

6. To fill in the remaining areas I used a glass cutter to cut thin strips of glass to glue on vertically. I nipped each piece to size.

7. Grout is optional. I used black grout to even out the pieces and give it a more finished look (Figure 6.11). If you would like the light to shine through the cracks, leave it as it is.

8. Light with tea candles or small battery-operated lights (Figure 6.12).

Figure 6.11
I finished this piece with black grout.

Figure 6.12
The colors look so rich when lit from within.

INSTRUCTIONS FOR TEALIGHT VOTIVE #2

1. Choose a large glass piece as a focal point to start. I used a rectangular glass "gemstone" with red glass beads radiating out from the center (Figure 6.13).

2. Use the same adhesive as in the first votive example. Glue your focal point in place and let dry.

3. Fill in the entire votive with random pieces of glass. You can fit them like a puzzle and nip when needed. I used blue glass and small contrasting beads to fill in the gaps (Figure 6.14). You can do it like this or plan a pattern with specific shapes and a variety of colors. I enjoyed filling in the space like a puzzle without having to plan or think about a design. This allowed me to quiet my mind.

Figure 6.13 This votive design features a large rectangular focus and small red glass beads radiating from it.

Figure 6.14 I filled in the rest of the votive with blue glass and small beads.

Figures 6.15 and **6.16** White grout makes the glass pieces stand out.

4. Grout if desired. I used dark glass, so I chose white grout to make the pieces stand out (Figures 6.15 and 6.16).

5. Light with tea candle or battery-operated light (Figure 6.17).

Figure 6.17
Illuminate the votive with a real or battery-operated tea candle.

Challenges and Variations

There are no limits to designing a miniature candle votive. You can cover the entire surface with strings of beads or make a patchwork design using random scraps as in the paperweight project. Don't forget holiday themes using pumpkins, hearts, Christmas colors, or Easter eggs. If you enjoy being precise, challenge yourself by making a measured geometric design. You can also choose to create a representational scene like a miniature sunset or underwater scene with fish. I have several friends who fell in love with these votives when I had some decorating my house over the holidays. I had one friend who was visiting from out of town and asked me to teach her how to make a votive right there and then. She had never worked with glass mosaic, but after a few pointers on nipping and gluing, she was hooked. She used the glass scrap patchwork approach and decided not to grout it to allow more light through (Figure 6.18).

Figure 6.18 Glass votive by Nancy Hays.

SERENITY STONES

For this project you will use smooth stones that you can fit in the palm of your hand. The weight of the stone may give you a sense of feeling grounded and calm. Create a mosaic design on one side of the stone for a visual effect. The other side of the stone is left smooth for you to caress in your palm or to rub with your thumb for the purpose of relaxation or anxiety relief. The process of creating a miniature mosaic on the stone and the finished product with its visual and tactile benefits are intended to provide serenity.

MATERIALS
- Smooth river stone that fits in the palm of your hand
- Opaque glass scraps
- Adhesive
- Grout

INSTRUCTIONS

1. Decide on colors and a design. The shape of the stone may suggest what design will work best. Use a round stone for creating a spiral.

2. Draw a spiral line with glue directly on the stone, leaving empty space as you spiral out. If the surface is flat, you can use liquid adhesive from a small bottle such as Gorilla Glue (Figure 6.20). If the surface is more curved, follow step 2 in the Instructions for Tealight Votive # 1 (page 62) to apply glue line.

3. Place small bits of glass on the glue line to form your first spiral (Figure 6.21).

4. Repeat steps 2 and 3 with another color (Figure 6.22).

5. Keep adding colors until the space is full. Three colors fit nicely on a palm-size stone (Figure 6.23).

6. Grout to match the stone (Figure 6.24).

Figure 6.19 Choose a smooth round river stone for a spiral design.

Figures 6.20 and **6.21** Draw a spiral line on the rock with glue and place your glass pieces.

Figure 6.22 Add the next row of your spiral in the same way.

Figure 6.23 Finish filling in your stone with glass as desired.

Figure 6.24 Grout to match the stone.

INSTRUCTIONS FOR BUTTERFLY OR NATURE-INSPIRED SERENITY STONE

1. Use this butterfly example or choose any simple animal, flower, leaf, or shell.

2. Sketch the basic shape of a butterfly or other small object or start directly using glue lines.

3. For the butterfly, cut a vertical sliver of glass for the body and glue in place (Figure 6.25).

4. Glue small slivers for antennae and then radiate out with colored scraps to fill the wings (Figure 6.26). You can use as many colors as you wish and make spots with round beads. Keeping it simple will work well on a small stone.

5. Grout to match the stone (Figure 6.27).

Figure 6.25 Cut a vertical sliver of glass for the butterfly body and glue in place.

Figure 6.26 Add antennae and wing pieces.

Figure 6.27 Grout to match the stone.

Challenges and Variations

You can expand your design to cover the entire surface of the front of your rock, as in the two examples by Emory Knott in Figures 6.28 and 6.29. Consider larger stones to place outside to create a serenity garden. Nestle decorated stones among plants along a garden pathway or around your favorite seating area. Figure 6.30 shows some designs on larger stones by Lenore Benitez.

Emory Knott used a small piece of slate, which gave her a flat surface, to create a hummingbird that can be placed in a garden or hung on a wall (Figure 6.31).

Figures 6.28 and **6.29** River rocks with entire tops covered in glass by Emory Knott

Figure 6.30 Designs on larger rocks by Leonore Benitez. You can add glass mosaics to any relatively flat rock.

Figure 6.31
Hummingbird on slate
by Emory Knott

MINIATURE LOCKETS, PENDANTS, AND WATCHES

How small do you want to go? Search for lockets, pendants, and watches that have a recessed area to place small shards of glass and glass beads. You may want to use tweezers for this project. You can glue and grout the pieces in place or use a two-part resin as in the first project in this section. These pieces can be worn as jewelry or displayed in shadow boxes individually or in groupings.

Emory's first mosaic was the hummingbird on slate (Figure 6.31). After that she began working smaller and smaller (Figures 6.32, 6.33, 6.34, 6.35, 6.36, 6.37, 6.38, and 6.39).

Figures 6.32, 6.33, 6.34, 6.35, 6.36, 6.37, 6.38, and **6.39** Using the techniques you have learned, you can use tiny shards of glass to create beautiful jewelry.

CHAPTER 7

FULL-SIZE WINDOWS

◇◇◇◇◇◇◇◇◇◇◇◇◇◇◇◇

If you like the beauty of old window sashes and the joy of working large, then full-size window projects are for you. This is my favorite way to work with mosaic stained glass and where I began my transparent stained glass journey. These projects do not require any more technical ability than the smaller projects, but might feel more advanced in design and composition, so the project instructions will focus on these concepts. It will also take longer to finish a window than one of the smaller projects. Once you start cutting and piecing glass you may become absorbed in the process, in a state of rhythm and calm. If you have a place to leave your project set up, you can take short breaks from the stressors of life and work on your window as time allows. If these ideas excite you, skip directly to this chapter after reading about materials and techniques. If you would like to practice first, try any number of the smaller projects in this book.

Your first challenge will be to find old windows. I acquired quite a collection by asking around and through my neighborhood websites. When homeowners replace windows in their houses, the old ones typically end up in the trash. People are usually willing to give their old windows away for free to be repurposed rather than having them end up in a landfill. Contractors may also be helpful in that way. If you need to look further, go to yard sales in older neighborhoods, construction dumpsters, alleyways, antiques stores, or building supply salvage warehouses. For example, in Baltimore there is a nonprofit retail center called Second Chance that sells building materials from deconstructed homes. There may be places like this in many other cities.

Completed windows can be displayed in front of other windows, along staircases, or as room or porch dividers.

NIP AND SHARDS WINDOWS

The three windows featured here were made by using scraps of glass and a wheel glass nipper. A glass cutter was not used. With this technique, the shapes of small glass pieces may suggest a design. Nipping off corners or edges will help shape the pieces to your liking. This is a fun way to be spontaneous and make up a design as you go along. If you are working with shards and scraps, it may be harder to use a preplanned drawing because you might not have the right shapes and colors to complete your design. Instead, have fun letting the existing shapes guide the way.

MATERIALS

- An old window with divided panes; no worries about peeling paint, old hardware, or cords
- Sandpaper and paints for preparing window sashes
- Glass shards or pieces in a variety of shapes and colors
- Wheel glass nippers
- Clear adhesive
- Grout
- Safety glasses and mask
- Small hooks to hang the windows with fishing wire, decorative chains, or cords. Check the packages to make sure the hardware can support the weight of the windows. If hanging the windows outside, consider securing the bottom corners of the window with fishing line to stabilize the window in the wind.

INSTRUCTIONS FOR FLORAL WINDOW

1. Select a window divided into rectangular panes.

2. Prepare the window sash. Old windows come in various conditions of disrepair. Peeling paint may contain lead and window hardware can be cumbersome or rusty. These features may also add character to your piece, so decide what you want to keep, alter, or remove. I had one commission where the client wanted the sashes to remain as they were. They were from his house and over a hundred years old. He wanted them to be left with peeling paint and the original hardware. I recommended sealing the paint with a clear coat of urethane for safety reasons.

Figure 7.1 Completed floral window

For this floral window I sanded the loose paint. I worked outside on a drop cloth while wearing a disposable mask to protect against lead dust. I used artist's oil paints to dry brush some color into the wood to blend and balance out the colors and to seal the old paint. You can use leftover house paint or stains and play around with brushing, dabbing, or wiping the paint with a rag. I left the window latch on as a fun and authentic detail.

3. Select your glass. You can use leftover scraps from other projects. This window was my first glass project, so I ordered colored scraps by weight on eBay. I was able to find a variety of small sheets of inexpensive green glass online too. Since most of my glass was green, I decided to do a floral design, thinking that the greens would work well in the background.

4. Choose some glass pebbles or nip glass circles for centers of flowers. I had some large round floral ceramic tiles that I had made for a ceramic mosaic and decided to use a few of them even

Figure 7.2 Keep the parts of the original window that you like.

though I knew that light wouldn't pass through them. Be creative with your choice of flower centers. Different textures and thicknesses will work well. Try glass pebbles, beads, or old costume pearls or gemstones for variety of texture (Figures 7.3, 7.4, 7.5, 7.6, and 7.7).

Figures 7.3, 7.4, 7.5, 7.6, and **7.7** I used glass beads, pebbles, and gems to make each flower center unique.

Figure 7.8 Some flowers may flow across dividers to maintain a continuity of design.

5. Arrange flower centers throughout the panes, leaving room for petals and stems. Think about each pane being its own composition but try to get balance and flow throughout the entire window. Allowing some of the flowers to flow into two panes can bring continuity to the composition while adding balance and interest to an individual panel (Figure 7.8).

6. Arrange glass pieces in patterns rotating out from the centers. Flowers are not perfectly symmetric so have fun playing with the shapes and angles of the petals. Nip the petals as desired to fit and form more pleasing shapes.

7. When you are satisfied with the arrangement of flowers, glue them in place.

8. Choose one color of green for the stems. Nip the glass into irregular rectangular segments to make curvy stems that connect and wind around the flowers. Add leaves in areas needed to fill some background space.

9. Glue stems and leaves.

10. Use a contrasting color for the background. I used dark green glass pieces of similar color but different textures.

11. Piece and glue the background in place.

12. Grout the window. Black grout will give the window a traditional stained glass look, but you can choose any color you like.

INSTRUCTIONS FOR ZOOM-INSPIRED WINDOW

Most people have become well acquainted with the concept of meeting with others virtually through Zoom. If you work from home, viewing clients and coworkers in a neat orderly grid on your computer screen may be a daily occurrence. Imagine having some fun with this idea by creating your own grid of whimsical faces by using the panes of a window.

1. Follow steps 1 through 3 in the instructions for the Floral Window on pages 72–73. For this window I used the glass that was left over from the floral window.

2. Arrange and nip pieces to create a face in each pane. Drawing ability is not needed for this task, and it will be easier if you don't overthink it. I wanted to use the glass I already had so I abandoned any idea of using a realistic color scheme and had the freedom to enjoy making a green nose, blue skin and lips, etc. Start by choosing shapes that may resemble facial features. The shapes can be as wacky as you want. If you have eyes, nose, and mouth your image will look like a face. Choose one basic color for the skin tone and fill in around the features. Think about eyebrows, ears, teeth, and glasses to

Figure 7.9 Completed Zoom-inspired window

individualize the faces (Figures 7.10 and 7.11).

3. Add other materials for embellishment if you choose. I used leftover faux pearls for teeth on one face and ceramic hand tiles for a couple of the others (Figures 7.12 and 7.13). Remember, light will not pass through these other materials.

4. Glue pieces as soon as you get a facial expression that satisfies you.

5. Continue working around the faces to add hair, hats, shirt collars, and jewelry. Don't be afraid to allow parts of one person to flow into the next pane.

6. Pick one background color for continuity or a different background for each pane to go for the Zoom effect of framing each face separately.

7. Glue all remaining glass pieces.

8. Grout the window. This example is grouted in black.

Figures 7.10 and **7.11** Start by choosing shapes that resemble facial features and make eyes, nose, and mouth. Colors do not need to be realistic.

Figures 7.12 and **7.13** Keep your mind open to other materials you may use in your mosaics. Here I used a ceramic tile in the shape of a hand and faux pearls for teeth.

INSTRUCTIONS FOR SUNSET WINDOW

1. Select a window. For this project I was fortunate enough to find a window with diagonal panes. These are difficult to come by but there is no problem with creating a sunset on a window with rectangular panes.

2. Prepare the sash. The window in this example was painted white and in good condition, so I left it as it was. If you want to repaint your sash use primer with latex paint or oil-based house paint. Old windows are typically painted with oil-based paint and latex can peel off if not primed first. Use exterior paint if you plan to hang your window outside.

3. Select your glass pieces. Warm colors such as yellows, oranges, reds, and pinks work well. The whole sky can be warm, or you can fill in with blues and purples. This sunset was inspired by some random pieces I had lying around. The center of the sun is a thick piece of red glass from a broken candle votive. The spiraling white rays are plastic, not glass, and come from a broken string of Christmas icicle lights.

4. A sunset composition can be made up of three basic components: sun, sky, and ground/water. Sunsets are varied, depending on setting, perspective, and weather (Figures 7.15, 7.16,

Figure 7.14 Completed sunset window

7.17, 7.18, 7.19, and 7.20). Decide where you want to put the horizon. If you want a large foreground, place the horizon high in the composition. If you want mostly sky, lower the horizon. The sun will be the focal point. Choose or create a rounded form for the sun. Place it at or near the horizon line. Glue it in place.

5. Add rays to the sun if you wish or begin to fill in streaks or cloud shapes of various colors in the sky.

6. Select colors and shapes to represent mountains, meadows, or water beneath the horizon.

7. Glue the remaining pieces.

8. Grout the window. The grout and sash of this window example are white. They appear darker because the photo is backlit.

Figures 7.15, 7.16, 7.17, 7.18, 7.19, and **7.20** Study sunset photos for a sense of the colors, perspective, and mood you want to portray.

CUT GLASS WINDOWS

Adding a glass cutter to the tools listed previously will allow for more precision in cutting particular shapes for a planned or spontaneous design. Using sheets of glass in addition to shards or scraps will allow enough area to cut the shapes and sizes of your choice. Refer to Cutting Glass Sheets in the Materials and Techniques chapter of this book for a refresher course on how to cut glass.

INSTRUCTIONS FOR GRAPEVINE WINDOW

The panes of a divided glass window may resemble the pattern on a trellis (Figures 7.22 and 7.23). Creating a grapevine twisting, turning, and cascading through the panes resembles grapevines growing on a trellis. The forms lend well to working spontaneously.

Figures 7.22 and **7.23** The panes of a divided glass window lend themselves well to mimicking a trellis.

Figure 7.21 Completed grapevine window

1. Select a window. For this project I was fortunate enough to find a window with diagonal panes. A window with rectangular panes would also work perfectly since many trellises have a rectangular pattern.

2. Prepare the sash. This window sash was originally white. I painted it with an exterior black enamel. I didn't like the smoothness and shine of the finish, so I hand sanded the surface to give the wood a more distressed appearance. Subtle hints of white are visible along some of the edges.

3. Decide on the colors of glass you would like to use. Grapes grow in an array of colors such as reds, purples, and greens. Since the leaves are typically green, I chose red for the grapes. Red and green are complementary colors and placing opposite colors next to each other helps them to look bolder and brighter. For a more subtle effect you can use different shades of green for the grapes and the leaves. Choose whatever color you like for the background. I picked amber tones to give the window a warm glow. Experiment by placing different colors next to what you have chosen for the grapes and leaves.

4. Cut round or oval shapes for the grapes. To cut circular shapes, start with a square or rectangle. Using a Sharpie marker, draw a circle or oval on the rectangle, touching the edges (Figure 7.24). Cut off the corners in arcs. Glass does not tend to break around tight curves easily so don't worry if your cuts end up mostly straight (Figure 7.25). Use the wheel nippers to round out the form (Figure 7.26). Remove any remaining Sharpie marker lines with alcohol or hand sanitizer.

5. The grape shapes should all be slightly different. You can use an occasional glass pebble of similar color to provide more variety in shape and texture. Arrange the grapes in clumps throughout the window. Any given clump can cross a window divide (Figure 7.27). Save a few extra grapes or partial/broken grapes to give the appearance of depth with the grapes overlapping. Use other partial grapes to peek out from behind leaves.

Figure 7.24 First draw your round shapes with a Sharpie marker.

Figure 7.25 It is difficult to cut curved lines in glass, so start by making straight ones.

Figure 7.26 Use wheel nippers to round out the form.

6. Glue down the grapes when you are pleased with the arrangement.

7. Draw leaf shapes on the glass and use the glass cutter to cut around the leaves and to divide them into sections both for aesthetic purposes and ease of cutting. Another way to make leaves is to use scraps and piece them together to form leaf shapes. The more variety you get in the shapes, the more natural and interesting the grapevine will look. Leaves should not look like they came from a cookie cutter.

8. Cut curvy segments to piece together to form the vines. Cut the ends of the segmented pieces on an angle when needed to form curls in the vines.

9. Arrange the leaves and vines together to cascade down between the clumps of grapes.

10. Glue when ready.

11. Fill in the background by cutting and nipping pieces of glass to fit. To follow the curve of a leaf or a vine, lay a piece of glass over the edge you want to fit it against and trace the line with a Sharpie marker. Cut along the line and the background piece should fit like a puzzle.

12. Glue the background in place.

13. Grout in the color of your choice.

Figure 7.27 Having some of your clumps of grapes cross over the trellis/ window dividers will add continuity to your design.

THE FOUR ELEMENTS WINDOWS: EARTH, AIR, FIRE, AND WATER

Sometimes the way the glass is divided can suggest a theme for a mosaic as in the Zoom and grapevine trellis windows. In this case I had two matching windows that were each divided into two panes. One window divided in half didn't speak to me, but the pair created interesting possibilities for a series of four. The theme could be based on an idea that is limited to four parts such as the seasons of the year or the suits in a deck of cards or you could create a theme using a subset of four of almost anything.

The example depicted here represents the four elements of matter that formed the foundation for many ancient beliefs. The ancient Greeks believed that all matter was comprised of earth, air, water, and fire. This theory was a basis for philosophy, science, and medicine for two thousand years. Today many mindfulness, meditation, and other wellness practices focus on the balance of these elements for mental and physical health. The four elements can be represented in physical or symbolic forms for different purposes. I chose to represent these elements in a window series for aesthetic reasons. I found the challenge of balancing one against the other energizing and visually exciting.

MATERIALS

- Old divided windows. This example uses two windows, each divided in half.
- Sandpaper and paints for preparing window sashes
- Safety glasses and mask
- Sheets and large pieces of transparent, colored glass, smooth or textured
- Glass cutter and nippers
- Clear adhesive
- Grout

Figure 7.28 The completed earth/air window

Figure 7.29 The completed fire/water window

INSTRUCTIONS

1. Select the windows. I was inspired by two windows that were each divided into two panes. You may choose or be limited to other options. One possibility could include creating the whole series on one window with panes divided into multiples of four, most commonly four or eight panels. You could also depict the elements on four separate windows. This would eliminate the fun of combining elements, but it would offer the flexibility of being able to juggle the order or arrangement of the display. This choice allows the opportunity for each window to stand alone or be part of the series.

2. Prepare the sashes. Wear a mask, eye protection, and gloves. Work outdoors or in a well-ventilated area to protect against lead dust exposure. These two windows had multiple layers of peeling paint and some rusty hardware. I removed the rusty pieces. I left the tarnished brass window latch on one window and an old piece of metal weatherstripping on the other to give each sash its own distinct detail. I used a handheld electric belt sander to remove loose paint and unevenly reveal the layers. I continued sanding until I was pleased with the distribution of bare wood, and green and white paint. The wood was smooth to the touch.

3. Sketch out some design ideas and decide how you want to group or pair the elements. Use realistic and symbolic photo references to

Figure 7.30 Allow the windows at your disposal to inspire your ideas. In this case, the four sections across two windows suggested the idea of a series.

Figure 7.31 Prepare the sashes by sanding and painting as desired.

Figures 7.32, 7.33, and **7.34** Study a variety of representations of the elements for ideas that will work well together.

give you ideas. Look at sky, ocean, flame, and weather pictures (Figures 7.32, 7.33, and 7.34). Study the movement of actual flames or running water. Figuring out how to translate images such as flames and air into glass pieces will require imagination and abstraction. After exploring many images, I decided to combine earth with air and fire with water. Copy my designs or create your own. The next set of instructions are for combining air and earth in one window.

4. Create a balanced design for earth and air. Land and sky go together well. The earth is the foundation of substance and nurturance. Your imagery may include rocks and dirt, hills or plains, with or without lifeforms. The earth symbolizes grounding, and the air is the connection to the universe. How do you want to combine these two elements? I wanted to depict a fluidity between the two elements. Rather than confining each element to its own pane of glass, you may allow the images to flow from one pane to the other while simultaneously having them each be the focus of one panel. The earth is the dominant image in the bottom pane, drawing attention to its bold rectangular shapes and solid forms. The air takes up a good bit of space in the bottom pane but is showcased in the upper panel with clouds and swirls. A plant emerges from the earth to literally bring life to the composition and connect the earth to the air in the top pane.

5. Once you have a small sketch or idea in your mind that you are satisfied with, make a sketch the size of your window. Place the window on a piece of paper that is slightly larger than the window. Trace the window and place marks indicating where the panes are divided. Set the window aside to work on the drawing. Use a ruler to draw lines across the window to mark the divides so you will know where the image is in relation to the individual panes. Now sketch the basic shapes of the design. Place the window back over the drawing to follow the design as you place your colored glass pieces (Figure 7.35).

Figure 7.35 Make a sketch and place it underneath your window to use as a guide for placing glass.

Figure 7.36 Select glass in a variety of shades, textures, and degrees of transparency.

6. Select the glass (Figure 7.36). Place different combinations of colored transparent glass together to form a pleasing palette. Use a variety of shades, textures, and degrees of transparency. Since air is clear you can represent it with the colors of the sky and clouds. You can also use a variety of textured clear glass.

Figure 7.37 Begin to glue your glass, starting with the main motifs.

Figure 7.38 I filled in the earth first, as it was the easier of the two elements.

7. Pick a focal point as a place to start piecing your glass. Trace your design by placing the colored glass directly on the window with the sketch underneath. I started with the plant because it is in the center of the composition and crosses both panes. Your drawing is there as a guide. You don't have to adhere to it exactly.

8. Cut the glass shapes using a glass cutter. I cut the leaves in half to replicate the center vein of the leaf as a detail. As an alternative, cut small triangles or nip existing shards to fill in the shapes with smaller pieces. Whichever way you prefer, make sure to leave small gaps between the pieces so the grout will enhance the details later. Make a stem by cutting curvy rectangular segments.

9. Glue the plant or other focal point once you are satisfied with its appearance and placement.

10. I used swirls to represent calm air movement. If you are using this symbol or other lines,

complete those next. You want to be able to adjust the line segments as you go so they are aligned and smooth. I used a variegated glass with pink, blues, and whites. The colors are subtle but different from the other colors I chose for the sky so they won't get lost in the design.

11. Cut swirls or lines in curvy segments. Again, you can trace the drawing or arrange small cut pieces directly along the lines. Sometimes cutting angled ends will be necessary to follow curves without them looking choppy.

12. Glue the lines in place and let dry (Figure 7.37). You now have enough of your design anchored down so pieces won't shift.

13. Next form the horizon line or the divide between earth and air. You can do this on either side of the line.

14. I filled in the earth first. For me it was the easier of the two elements and gave structure to the piece. I used brown and amber tones cut into rectangles. The rectangles are laid in rows following the curves of the two hills and glued in place (Figure 7.38).

15. The air was completed last. The paler shades appear at the horizon and the blues become brighter in the top pane. The sky tends to look bluer higher up and fade toward the horizon. This concept worked well to bring attention to the air in the top panel. I cut long curvy lines across sheets of blue glass and then cut the long shapes into smaller pieces, mixing different shades of blue. The shapes of the sky pieces, the clouds, and the swirls all contribute to the sense of movement of the air going across the window.

16. After getting a sense of how the window will look, glue the pieces in place (Figure 7.39).

Figure 7.39 The earth/air window with all glass placed

Figures 7.40 and **7.41** Study images of fire and water to understand their shapes and movement.

RANDY FARIS/THE IMAGE BANK VIA GETTY IMAGES

IRABELL/ISTOCK VIA GETTY IMAGES

17. Use the same process of planning, drawing, and selecting glass for the fire and water window. These two elements can be much more challenging than earth and air. Fire and water have a lot more movement and energy than earth and air. They are opposing forces that need to work together for the success of the piece. Yet that is the excitement of putting these elements together. Enough water will quench a fire, but too much fire will evaporate water. They shouldn't overpower each other or the other window. Study fire and water to understand the shapes and movement they take on (Figures 7.40 and 7.41). Notice flames have a concentration of yellows in the center of the shapes, surrounded by oranges and reds. Black in the background helps to define the shapes of the flames. To create as much energy in the water, look at wave patterns. Foamy whites define the tips of the waves and streaks of blue indicate the movement.

Figures 7.42, 7.43, and **7.44** Select your glass and set up your window on top of your sketch.

18. Select your glass and set up your window on top of your sketch (Figures 7.42, 7.43, and 7.44).

19. I started with water by cutting long curvy pieces out of glass and then shaping them to fit the curves in the wave pattern drawing. The foamy tips of the waves are defined with shards of white that were left over from the clouds in the previous window. Define one wave against the others by using darker shades of blue for the outlines. Remember the drawing is just a guide. Feel free to change the shapes of the waves as you piece the glass together.

20. Continue to cut pieces and glue glass until the water is completed. Notice the waves enter the top pane and the fire will intertwine with the water in the lower pane (Figure 7.45). As in the earth/air window, each element enters the opposing panel to create balance but allows the dominant element to be the focus within the pane.

Figure 7.45 Notice the waves enter the top pane and the fire will intertwine with the water in the lower pane.

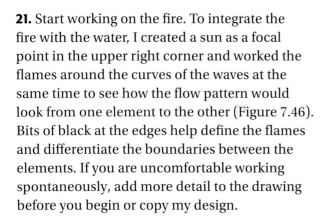

Figure 7.46 I started the fire section with a sun in the upper right corner and began to work flames around the curves of the waves.

Figure 7.47 All pieces are glued in the fire/water window.

21. Start working on the fire. To integrate the fire with the water, I created a sun as a focal point in the upper right corner and worked the flames around the curves of the waves at the same time to see how the flow pattern would look from one element to the other (Figure 7.46). Bits of black at the edges help define the flames and differentiate the boundaries between the elements. If you are uncomfortable working spontaneously, add more detail to the drawing before you begin or copy my design.

22. Glue as you feel satisfied. Continue working until the fire fills the remaining space (Figure 7.47).

23. Grout both windows at the same time. Consider how to choose the color. I would have preferred white for the air and earth window to give the air a lighter feeling, however I thought it was more important to use black for the flames to give an authentic fiery look. I wanted to use the same color grout on both windows for the continuity of the series so I chose black as the color that would work best with all the elements.

Nature Series Windows

Sometimes a single window can become a part of a series after the fact. In the beginning of the COVID-19 pandemic I responded to a post on a neighborhood website from a man offering to donate original windows from his one-hundred-year-old row home. He wanted them to be put to good use, so he asked me what I intended to do with them. I showed him a couple of photos of my work, and he commissioned me on the spot to create a mosaic on one of the larger windows he gave to me.

The client was going to be working from home for an indefinite period of time and wanted something beautiful and meaningful to look at in his third-floor home office. I asked him what he wanted on the window. He said he and his family only intended to live in Baltimore for a few years and then return to their roots in the Midwest. The client said he would like to take a piece of art back with him to remember his house in Baltimore. An original window would be a perfect souvenir. He said he liked nature and that it would be nice if the design included Black-Eyed Susans, the Maryland state flower. Otherwise, I could create whatever I wanted. Having free reign over the piece exhilarated me!

The window did not have divided panes to provide structure. I found the large expanse of a single panel to be both daunting and freeing. In creating the design, I followed the steps used in my Floral Window (page 72) by placing an arrangement of flowers throughout the window. Rather than using shards, I used the glass cutter to cut petal shapes specific to the Black-Eyed Susans. After placing the flowers, I added dragonflies and smaller white flowers for variety of size, shape, and color. I created a sense of flow throughout the piece by adding curvy stems as described in my other floral window. To provide a sense of landscape in the background, I used blues to represent sky in the top of the composition and gradually transitioned to greens for the ground (Figure 7.48).

Figure 7.48 Completed window, part of nature series

Figure 7.49 Nature series, day   **Figure 7.50** Nature series, night

After grouting and completing this window, it fell over and shattered. This was my first commissioned window, and I was devastated. But this story has a happy ending, which you can read about in the Materials and Techniques chapter of this book (page 3). My client was so elated by the window that he commissioned me to do two more to hang as a series. This time he said,

"Do whatever you want!" The idea came to me right away to flank each side of the large window by depicting day and night. From an aesthetic point of view, I knew this idea would give me the opportunity to carry through the floral nature theme using different settings and colors. Symbolically, the series represents the passage of time throughout a day (Figures 7.49, 7.50, and 7.51).

Figure 7.51 Completed nature trio hanging in windows

Love Is Forever: The Art of Remembrance Windows by Dan Patrell

Once you know the technical steps for creating a full-size window series, there is no limit to the depth of personal meaning and creativity that can be expressed in your windows. The more you search inward the greater the chance your art will be genuinely beautiful while leading to self-discovery and possibly personal healing. By following the instructions provided and the inspiration provided by Dan Patrell you can create a window series to represent your personal journey.

Following the passing of Connie Walker, Dan's wife of twenty-three years, in December 2013 (just six weeks after being diagnosed with ovarian cancer), Dan had a tugging need to honor his wife and all the beauty she created around her. He decided to make something to honor her inner beauty. The result was *Love Is Forever* (Figures 7.52, 7.53, 7.54, and 7.55), and this is his story.

In 2015 Dan's windows became a part of a yearlong exhibit at the American Visionary Art Museum (AVAM) in Baltimore's Inner Harbor called *The Big Hope*. The works featured are said to be "soulful creations reflecting personal transcendence." Coincidentally, AVAM was Connie's favorite museum. With its emphasis on self-taught artists, Dan and Connie loved visiting the museum to learn the stories behind the art, the struggle for expression and the messages crystalized in the work. "Knowing these windows containing her spirit resided there—perhaps to inspire the people who see them—must surely be making my sweetie smile," said Dan.

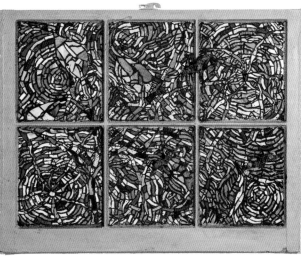

Figures 7.52, 7.53, 7.54, and **7.55** *Love Is Forever* series by Dan Patrell. PHOTOS BY MIKE MORGAN

I decided to create four mosaic windows for Connie's mother and siblings on matching old window frames with their glass still intact (five years earlier, I'd made my first mosaic for Connie's forty-fourth birthday). On top of each pane, I designed an image of swirling blue skies, a cascading sun, greenery, and finally, "bird wisps" mounted on two-inch posts. The bird wisps served a few purposes: One was to honor Connie's love of birds. Whenever she had a dream of flight, she'd tell me about it in earnest: where she'd soared, the exuberance, the freedom. She put up so many feeders in our yard that our porch was a feast for cardinals, wrens, finches, and others I could never identify. Many days, I'd find her sitting on our back porch with our old dog, Zed, watching birds darting in and out of the forsythia. These wisps, in addition to giving the works a three-dimensional feel, also signified the members of each family in each window.

But there are other messages embedded in the mosaic, as well: The sun's rays spell out, in Morse code, "love is forever," and my then thirteen-year-old daughter selected "healing stones," unique to each family, which I placed within each work. I also knew from the moment I conceived this project that Connie's ashes would be folded into the grout holding the mosaics together. For my daughter, Connie's family, and myself, I wanted to imbue my work with a sense of her spirit. The day I grouted was an emotional one, but it felt right.

I started the project in July 2014, as soon as the windows arrived, and finished five months later. Every day and evening were the same: get up, break glass, place it. Repeat. I worked at a steady pace and finished the day before Christmas Eve. On that final day, after cleaning myself up, I went outside to take stock of the windows again. Opening the garage door, with little light, I had a revelation. The force of it literally knocked me down, and I found myself sitting on the floor in a puddle of my own tears, but not sad ones: The windows I'd worked so hard on weren't just a gift from me; they were a gift from Connie. That realization sucked the air out of me and made me happier than I'd been since before she passed. I never imagined the act of making these windows would be a transformative experience and part of my ongoing healing, but it was.

—Dan Pattrell

Haiku (1): The Mindfulness Window by Dan Patrell

Haiku (1) is the first in a series of windows by Dan that explores a theme initiated by a selected haiku (Figure 7.56). Dan also calls this *The Mindfulness Window*. Over the course of making the *Love Is Forever* windows, he developed a daily practice of mindfulness meditation. He doesn't know how this process started but he thinks perhaps his wife's spirit guided him to this path. For this window, he set an intention to create a work that was meditative. A trip to Japan helped Dan determine that using a haiku as the basis for the window "felt absolutely right."

Thematic windows as described earlier can be made up of a series of any number of windows or within one window with each pane representing a segment of the series. *Haiku (1)* is the first of a theme depicting a haiku in a series that will provide Dan with countless options for future windows. The use of Japanese Kanji script in the design creates a series within the individual window by depicting at least one Kanji symbol

in each of the nine panes written up to down using correct Japanese grammar to complete the haiku. Each Kanji symbol is a work of art within itself to bring focus and importance to a particular panel. Since the haiku that Dan selected references bamboo, he created a field of bamboo surrounded by a swirling psychedelic sky. The colors in the sky itself emanate from the central panel with a burst of white that separates itself into various colors. Within each of these outside panels are three little pieces of gold mirror, each signifying a change for that color in the panel. Within each pane, the interplay between the colors differs, making them dependent and interdependent of the other. Here is the Haiku in Japanese, followed by the English translation:

.筍を見つめてござる「哉
staring at the shoots
of new bamboo . . .
Buddha

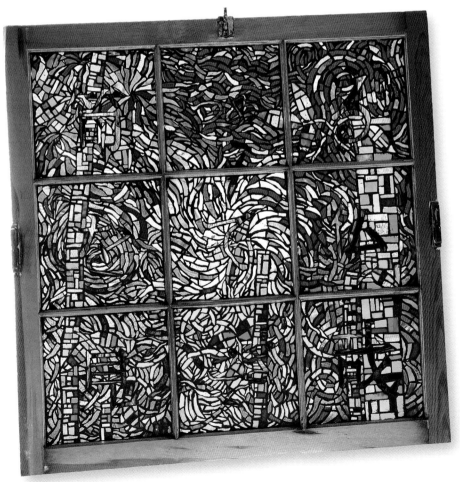

Figure 7.56
Haiku (1): The Mindfulness Window by Dan Patrell.

Challenges and Variations for Full-Size Windows

An artist's work can often be identified by a distinct style. The style in which a mosaic artist cuts and pieces glass may be as unique and distinct as a painter's brushstrokes on a canvas. For example, in Dan Patrell's *Love Is Forever* and *Mindfulness* windows, there is a distinct style similar to Impressionism where short strokes of different colors are formed by using multiple colors of freeform rectangular segments and curves to create an all-over pattern of movement and excitement. The colors are blended by the viewer's eye much like in an Impressionist painting.

You can choose to vary your technique by cutting or piecing your glass in an entirely different way than you did before. You can experiment by cutting a pile of glass in small uniform shapes, or go to the opposite extreme and make long freeform cuts across a new sheet of glass. Perhaps choose colors and textures that feel unfamiliar. While there is no mistaking *Love is Forever* and *Mindfulness* as being created by the same artist, *Wine Splash* (Figure 7.57) and *Hidden Heart* (Figure 7.58), also created by Dan Patrell, have a very different feel to them. In these two windows the glass shapes are cut in

precise rectangles and are placed in straight rows to form an all-over pattern. The colors are grouped homogeneously to form bold solid shapes of color that create movement through lines and patterns throughout the windows.

Perhaps you haven't tried any projects beyond the chapter on Quilt Pattern techniques because you are unable or not interested in cutting glass. Cutting glass is not a requirement for working on a full-size window. Jan Ross is a stained glass artist who shattered her elbow a couple of years ago. As a result of having an elbow replacement, she no longer has the strength nor steadiness to cut glass. This led her to finding another method of creating mosaic. The result is this beautiful window that adorns her front door (Figures 7.59, 7.60, and 7.61). Jan began by collecting glass pieces from thrift shops, dollar stores, or wherever she could find pieces of interest. She considers herself a serial shopper and had a blast going on scavenger hunts. She used coasters, small plates, trinkets boxes, small candlestick holders, and salt cellars. The cellars came from a collection she had plus a couple bought on eBay. The baubles came from

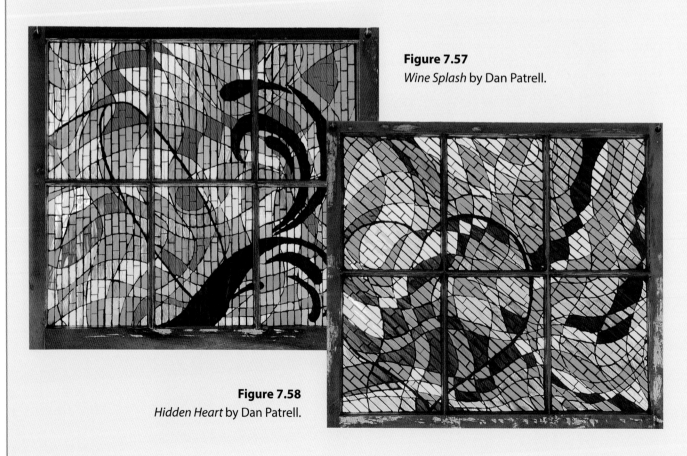

Figure 7.57
Wine Splash by Dan Patrell.

Figure 7.58
Hidden Heart by Dan Patrell.

Figures 7.59, 7.60, and **7.61**
Side light window by Jan Ross

Figure 7.62
My window inspired
by *Starry Night*

Hobby Lobby. Next, she had a friend cut ten glass panels to fit the existing window next to her front door. She designed the placement of glass pieces on the panels and glued them with E6000 transparent adhesive. She filled the remaining space by attaching baubles with fast-drying epoxy, and then used epoxy to attach the panels in place on her side light window. This technique will work well on freestanding old windows or, if you choose to be more daring, you could adhere your design directly onto your existing windows.

Jan's piece was not only created without cutting, but also without grouting. Remember this is an option for all your windows. I made an ungrouted window inspired by Vincent van Gogh's popular painting *Starry Night* (Figure 7.62). The clear glass gaps between the colored pieces create an entirely different look than a grouted piece.

CHAPTER 8

THE ARTISTS' STORIES

◇◇◇◇◇◇◇◇◇◇◇◇◇◇◇◇

This book begins with ways to set your intentions for creating stained glass mosaics. The artists represented throughout this text were motivated by the same ideas intended to motivate you. They are primarily self-taught, driven by a common desire for self-expression and exploration.

Emory Knott

The Mosaic Miniatures chapter was inspired by the work of Emory Knott. I met Emory in 2015 when she came to me to take what started as private drawing lessons with her cousin Luke. Emory and Luke attended separate schools and didn't have a chance to spend much time together. Since they both loved art, they used their weekly lessons as a special time to create and be together. Emory enjoyed exploring new media and had her own ideas of what to try next. Luke was up for just about anything, but he loved to sculpt and work with his hands. At the time I had been working on mosaics using ceramic tiles. They saw my work in the studio and asked if they could make a mosaic. I set Luke up with a piece of cement board and he worked out a design using ceramic and opaque tiles. Emory came to the lesson equipped with small bits of glass, nippers, tweezers, and glue. She had been introduced to the mosaic process in a workshop she attended with her mother. After Luke finished his mosaic, he stopped taking lessons to pursue sports and

other interests. Emory continued to take lessons until she graduated from high school. My mosaic experience had been with large ceramic pieces, while Emory preferred to work very small. I had never worked with glass (let alone tweezers), but Emory didn't want my help with techniques or ideas. What she needed was my support and a quiet space to pursue her art without judgment. She enjoyed talking about art or life in general. It wasn't until later that I realized I was providing Emory with the opportunity for mindfulness.

Emory likes the containment of small pieces. "I like to see the whole project when I'm making it," she explained. "If I get started on a big project, I hit a roadblock. It becomes hard to move forward because it seems like there is no end in sight." Emory is extremely detail oriented. She will maintain the same degree of detail whether she is working large or small, so the time component can be overwhelming with a larger piece.

Figure 8.1 Linoleum block printing by Emory Knott.

Emory's mosaics are very personal. She depicted scenes on themes ranging from the ocean to outer space to think about where her place is in the world. She then reflects to examine her struggles. Emory often created these miniature scenes in lockets and pendants so she could carry them around or wear them to keep them close.

Emory has since graduated from college with a degree in fine art. She hasn't worked with glass since high school, but she continues to work in miniature. Currently she is focused on small, detailed linoleum block printing and is selling her work online (Figure 8.1).

Leonor Benitez

In 2011, after returning from vacation, Leonor discovered that the glass top of her outdoor table had been broken in a storm. She looked into replacing it and found that it would cost $400 to buy a new one. Rather than pay that much money she thought, *I can make my own tabletop!*

She had never done mosaics but read about it and taught herself. She started with ceramic tiles (Figure 8.2).

Leonor was so happy with her table that she then made a bench and kept on going. She read and watched videos to learn about stained glass mosaics. She said, "I became addicted to the process right away. I need it. It is like a drug for me." She said it relaxes her, keeps her mood calm, and prevents depression.

Leonor had never made art or crafts before with only one exception. Leonor was born and raised in Cuba. Before immigrating to the United States in 1994 she spent a year in a refugee camp in Guantanamo Bay. She said there was nothing to do there, and she became very bored. She found a large piece of wood and, although she had no tools or experience, she decided to carve the wood to make a sculpture. Using a screwdriver and shark skin for sandpaper, she set to work. The finished piece was a large bird with its wings spread, perched on an outstretched human hand. Every feather was meticulously carved and sanded to a smooth finish. Leonor said the finished work weighed over seventy

Figure 8.2 The first mosaic by Leonor Benitez

pounds. It wasn't until seventeen years later that she made her first mosaic.

A mutual friend introduced Leonor to Meredith Ormsby. The friend recognized their common interest in stained glass and thought the two women would have much to share. They immediately bonded and remain close friends. When they met, Meredith was only doing traditional stained glass, which requires larger pieces of glass than used in mosaics. She was regularly giving her small scraps away to Leonor until Leonor convinced her to start making her own mosaics. Leonor taught Meredith what she knew and together they go on shopping sprees for glass and to thrift stores and yard sales for tables, vases, pots, and anything else they might be inclined to glue glass to. They sometimes exhibit and sell their work together while sharing many laughs and good times.

While working full time as a Spanish teacher, Leonor spent every available evening and weekend making mosaics. She took over her entire basement to use as a mosaic studio. In 2017 she left her teaching position for personal reasons. With more time available she gradually worked her way to making mosaics full time. She is motivated by the process and accumulates more pieces than she wants or needs. She sells her work at farmer's markets, fairs, and shops. She feels gratified when people want to buy things she created and is inspired by ideas that make others happy. She loves bright colors and themes in nature. She said anything that she makes with flowers will sell well.

Leonor plans to move to Florida in a few years when her husband retires. She wants to be in a warmer climate where she is surrounded by familiar culture, family, and friends. Her dream is to open a shop where she can teach and sell mosaics. She imagines a relaxed environment for people to gather, talk, and have fun together while sharing her love of creating mosaics.

I discovered Leonor's work at The Carriage House, a quaint neighborhood craft gallery in Roland Park, Baltimore. I had a few of my pieces on consignment alongside of Leonor's impressive collection of whimsical tables, lanterns, pots, and more. When I decided to write this book I contacted Leonor almost immediately, knowing she would be a great inspiration to all.

Meredith Ormsby

Meredith has always enjoyed making things. She started her college education by spending two years as an art major concentrating on

Figure 8.3 Irises by Meredith Ormsby, her most cherished piece

photography and drawing but ultimately earned a bachelor's degree in business and advertising. Her love for creating and helping others motivated her to return to school for a master's degree in occupational therapy. In graduate school she learned about making traditional crafts. She loved working with children and the process of making something from nothing. Through the joy of creating, she helped her clients overcome physical challenges by learning to cut, color, and hold a pencil. In 2019, while working with adults in home health care, Meredith injured her back and tore her rotator cuff. Since her work in home care required heavy lifting and physical exertion, she had to rely on disability insurance. She continues to treat a few children and one or two adults privately, but her practice is very limited. The silver lining in this loss is that Meredith has more time to pursue her own crafts.

In 2015, while Meredith was still working full time, she was looking for something creative to do after her son went away to college. She started taking classes in stained glass and loved the craft. She made so much art that she began selling her stained glass at a local farmer's market and then expanded to shows and then juried shows. She decided to make a business out of it and considered it "a good side gig" while she was still working full time. She continues to do shows but, due to her injury, she needs help setting up and dismantling her booth.

Meredith met Leonor at the farmer's market through a mutual friend two years after she started working in stained glass. She was happy to give Leonor her leftover scraps of glass but could not be convinced to use the glass herself to make mosaics. It took several years for Leonor to coax Meredith to give it a try.

Meredith uses her unfinished basement as her work and storage space. She said mosaics still feel new to her. She welcomes the change in mindset and process, but also continues to enjoy traditional stained glass methods. She likes to work in large blocks of time and has several projects going at once. By multitasking she can make the best use of her time moving from one task to another. She is a self-proclaimed hoarder and is motivated by what she has on hand.

Meredith must sell her work to make space to create more. There is only one piece she will not part with. Meredith was working with a woman in home health care, and she began to bring in suncatchers she had made to cheer up her client. This motivated Meredith to make her a larger piece. She created a stained glass panel of irises as a special gift. After Meredith's client passed away, her family returned the irises to Meredith, and it remains her most cherished piece (Figure 8.3).

Dan Patrell

Through Dan's background in editing and writing, he has learned the value of a story. Dan published a magazine on Maryland art and culture. His work frequently took him to Maryland's Eastern Shore where he befriended a mosaic artist. Dan had never set out to be an artist himself and he claims that if you asked him to draw or paint something he would fail miserably. So, when his friend invited him to make a mosaic, he wasn't sure how he could do this with the amount of skill and time needed. His friend reassured him that when he was in the area he could take as much time as he liked to complete the process. Dan agreed to make a mosaic. He learned he could use art to tell a story and he has cherished that intention ever since. Dan described this process in his own words.

"My first window, a bird on a branch, was going to be a birthday gift for my wife, Connie. Over the course of several trips to the Eastern Shore I would cut glass pieces and secure them. I found the process meditative—and still do, which is one of the big appeals to me. During one visit, as I cut some glass, I cut my fingertip. It wasn't a big deal; it happens a lot in mosaics. As I was watching the bead of blood get larger on my fingertip, I was thinking, *I really should get a bandage*, but then I looked at an empty space on my window and remembered that this is for Connie. So, I gave the finger a good shake, and the blood dropped on the window. After letting it dry, I sealed it by gluing a glass piece atop of it, trapped like a bug in amber. Later, when I

Figures 8.4 Dan Patrell's first mosaic, made for his wife Connie

Figure 8.5 Dan Patrell with *Love Is Forever* (see page 91).

PHOTOS BY MIKE MORGAN

presented the window to Connie, I pointed out the blood behind the yellow-colored glass. I told her, 'For whatever might happen in the future, now you have my DNA to convict me.' Eight months later, for Christmas, Connie converted our garage into a mosaic studio for me.

The concept of story in my works is very important to me. Most of my pieces involve Morse code of some kind. In my *Love is Forever* windows, a traditional form of Morse code (dots and dashes) can be seen in the sun's rays cutting through each window. The Morse code spells out, 'love is forever.' My preferred use of Morse code, however, is not through dots and dashes, but through color, where dots are represented in one color, dashes are another, and a third color is used as a spacer between the letters. A First Amendment vase I created spells out the entire First Amendment of the US Constitution, using this method of Morse code. The project I am currently working on will have the message embedded into the colors of the petals of flowers. In this regard, the message is there, but it's sort of subversive.

I do these mosaics because I enjoy the process. It truly is meditative. If I am not careful, I could head out to the garage and stay there for hours, losing track of time. I do it because I have something I truly want to say. Each window takes a while to complete. I must think about the project for quite some time before it solidifies in my head. It needs to be meaningful for me to invest an unlimited number of hours on a major project. I do it because I like the voice that comes from it. Yes, I am a writer, but I get more enjoyment when I can 'write' with glass."

Jan Ross

While growing up, Jan Ross never considered herself artistic. It was not until she was in her twenties that she first became aware of her creativity. Her career path led her to a position as a regional program administrator for Rockwell International, which she described as "a very stressful left-brained job." Jan needed a creative outlet and a way to relax. She had always loved glass, so she decided to take a class in stained

Figure 8.6 Glass mosaic by Jan Ross

glass. Her first project was a five-foot half-moon Victorian window. Jan was amazed at how motivated she was to make art. She became a jewelry maker and taught herself the art of fused glass, which she uses in making fabricated sterling jewelry instead of gems. She sold her jewelry for many years by doing shows on the weekends. Jan enjoys learning all sorts of new crafts such as metal art, pottery, and woodworking. Since she retired, she has more time to devote to her art and always has a project in the works. She is motivated to find new ways to work with her favorite materials. Her window featured in this book was the first piece she created when she was no longer able to cut glass.

Robin M.N. Jones

From the first time I was able to hold a crayon, I started making art and never stopped, but I hadn't cut or nipped a piece of glass until a few years ago. When I was growing up visual expression came easily to me, and my parents nurtured and supported my passion every step of the way. I found challenge in reaching new skill levels and trying new media. I try to take advantage of what is available to me given opportunities and limitations. In college as a sculpture major, I cast as much bronze as I could, knowing I might not have access to a foundry after I graduated.

After completing a master's degree in art therapy, I encountered a bit of artist's block. My mentor once told me that if you get stuck, change your media entirely to start fresh without previous expectations. I took his advice and taught myself quilt making. This was an effective creative and practical change, as I was just married, living in a small apartment without a studio, and focusing on a new career as an art therapist.

It was through practicing art therapy that I truly learned the power of artistic expression. The art process can provide access to thoughts and feelings that verbal expression cannot. Through art therapy I helped to facilitate positive changes in individuals of all ages and challenges. I've worked with children as young as two years old on up to seniors with challenges, including physical, social/emotional, psychiatric, and physical/sexual trauma. A guided therapeutic art process can help provide support, insight, coping skills, and improved self-esteem.

Over the years of providing art therapy and private art instruction, I have witnessed

Figure 8.7 Mosaic by Robin M. N. Jones

extraordinary growth, change, and beauty in others that has motivated me in my own artistic pursuits. My greatest improvement in painting occurred when I opened a studio to teach art to children, teens, and adults. They were inspired by my example and wanted to see what I was working on at any given time. I had an audience expecting me to produce, and my painting improved greatly during that time.

In 2008 I had a major life change. My husband made a career choice that moved us from Virginia Beach to Baltimore after seventeen years. I closed my beloved studio, we sold our house, and the second of our two children went off to college. I had a completely fresh start with the freedom to do as I pleased. The scope of possibilities felt exciting but overwhelming to me as I set up my easel, applied for jobs, and did volunteer work.

It was time to get a new start with art making too. I enrolled in a class at a community ceramic studio for basic wheel. I had made a few attempts at throwing pots years ago but never had the proper instruction. Once I learned that I needed to spin the wheel in reverse because I was lefthanded, I was able to progress without frustration. While at the studio I took interest in mosaic murals made of handmade ceramic tiles and pottery shards that were hung on the walls of the studio and in the bathrooms. I jumped at the opportunity to take a two-day workshop on basic materials and techniques for making a mosaic. I decorated the frame of a mirror with broken pottery pieces that were available at the studio. Sometime after that experience I bought glass tiles in various colors and spent my free time over the summer making an octopus table on an old tree stump in my yard (see page 41). The sculptor in me wanted more. I took a few more pottery classes after that so I could have access to the studio and kiln to make my own tiles. I made faces, birds, flowers, leaves, squiggles, and any other shape and textured tile I could think of. I used these tiles to create mirror frames and a

series of wall mandalas until I exhausted my supply of handmade tiles and felt satisfied to move on to something different.

I always had an interest in learning traditional stained glass methods, but somehow this never happened. With a recent interest in mosaics and a love for stained glass, I thought the best direction to take would be to combine these ideas as I had seen other artists do. I don't remember how I acquired my first window, but I must have been on the lookout. As explained in the Full-size Windows chapter, I ordered glass scraps online and set to work on my first stained glass project. I delighted in the process and the outcome and continue to this day.

The opportunity to write this book couldn't have come at a better time. Schools and businesses were shut down due to the COVID-19 pandemic. My art therapy position did not translate well to a virtual platform, causing my work to become difficult and frustrating for me and my clients. My private art lessons had dwindled down to one student who I taught in person. Meanwhile, I had developed a new skill set for an exciting craft that I could teach to all levels of students, and I needed an accessible way to deliver the instruction. I approached the idea of teaching through a book as a new form of expression and communication in the way I approach working with a new art medium, excited by the challenge and opportunity. The shift felt strange to me since I was used to teaching by interacting with my students and offering immediate encouragement and feedback. For the book I had to create examples and provide step-by-step instructions while trying to imagine the progress and setbacks my students would encounter without having met them. I am not accustomed to teaching in a rote manner, so I tried to offer examples and methods that encourage creative processes and individualized thinking rather than formulaic results. I was pleasantly surprised at how much I enjoyed and learned from this experience.

RESOURCES

◇◇◇◇◇◇◇◇◇◇◇◇◇◇◇

These are the glass stores in my area that I recommend. Glass tiles can also often be found at big-box hardware and home stores. If you can't find a source nearby for what you need, online options abound.

Maryland Mosaics, LLC
https://www.marylandmosaics.com/
11521 Cronridge Dr. Ste. G
Owings Mills, MD 21117
(410) 356-3555
Great for all types of opaque ceramic and glass mosaic tiles.

Anything Stained Glass
anythinginstainedglass.com
5104 Pegasus Ct.
Frederick, MD 21704
(800) 462-1209
Best selection of sheet glass, tools. Good prices. Variety of scrap bins.

The Artist's Corner
https://artistscornerstainedglass.com/
7524 Belair Rd.
Baltimore, MD 21236
(410) 665-4633
Glass sheets, tools.

ACKNOWLEDGMENTS

◇◇◇◇◇◇◇◇◇◇◇◇◇◇◇

Thank you to the artists who contributed to the making of this book: Dan Patrell, Leonor Benitez, Emory Knott, Meredith Ormsby, and Jan Ross. I hope their rich stories and beautiful artwork will inspire readers as much as they have inspired me.

Thank you to my dear lifelong friends, Sharon Hernes Silverman and Nancy Scheller Hays. Sharon, a friend from high school, seemed to appear out of nowhere to plant the seed for this book. She gave me initial guidance and connected me to her publisher. Nancy has been a continual inspiration since graduate school. She offers unconditional support and enthusiasm toward my ideas and was my test case student for trying out one of the projects in this book. I look forward to seeing her complete them all.

My deepest gratitude goes to my husband, Steven R. Jones, who has always provided me with the mental and physical space to pursue my every dream. In addition, he expertly photographed my hands and face for this book and has tolerated countless glass splinters that relentlessly find their way to his feet.